THE
WISE
BOUDOIR

A Journey of Love and Intimacy from The Far Side of 50

LIV WRIGHT

Copyright © 2024 The Wise Boudoir by Liv Wright

All rights reserved.

PUBLISHER'S NOTE

Printed in the United States of America. No part of this publication may be reproduced, distributed, or transmitted in any form or by any means, including photocopying, recording, video, streaming, or by mechanical methods, without the prior written permission of the publisher, except in the case of brief quotations embodied in critical articles and reviews. For permission requests, contact the publisher Prete, LLC, 5000 Thayer Street, Oakland, MD 21550.

ISBN: 979-8-218-34768-0

Table of Content

FORWARD 7
INTRODUCTION 1
PART ONE 6
   DATING, MATING, AND PARTNERING AFTER 50 6
      Mature Marriage: Mandela and Machel 7
      Whose Couch is Gonna Be Thrown Out? 12
      The Magic Mirror – Our Lovers, Ourselves 15
      Sadie Hawkins 2.0 19
      Money and the Baby-Boomer Boudoir 22
      Our Gin Game 25
      Because with Him I Feel All "Girly" 28
      Flirt! 32
      On Savoring and Being Savored 35
      Are We Fighting About *That* Again? 38
      What Love Looks Like to Us Now 41
      Partnered at 60 46
      Getting to Know You: Then and Now 49
      Will You Still Need Me, Will You Still Feed Me, When I'm 64? ... 52
      He Loves Me, He Loves Me Not 55
      In What Ways are You Crazy? 59
      Gratefulness and Intimacy 62
PART TWO 65
   SEX AFTER 50 65
      Booty Call? But Sir, I'm 70, Black, and Disabled! 66
      Jet Lag, Cut Flowers, and the "Little Blue Pill" 70
      Condoms, Anyone? 74

    Sex Ed for Grownups, or Who Knew? 78

    Make My Toes Curl, You Rascal You! 81

    Have Fun and Go Shopping for Some Sex Toys, People! 84

    Am I Hopelessly Square, or What? 88

    "Sex Without "Sex" 92

    Making Sex Easy for Everyone 95

    Do I Really Have to Go into a Nursing Home to Get Some Action? 100

    Looking for New Christmas Moves? 103

    Romance 2.0 106

    Love Me Tender 110

PART THREE 113

  A LOOK IN THE REARVIEW MIRROR 113

    Where Were You When Slow Dancing Died? 114

    The Music that Made Us Dance: Baby-Boomer Love Songs 101 117

    Will There Ever Be Love Songs Again? 121

    Coming of Age before Roe and the Pill 126

    Wild and Crazy Sex between the Pill and the Virus 129

    Prince Charming Stories 133

    An Auld Lang Syne Salute to My New Year's Eve Marriage Proposals 140

PART FOUR 143

  OUR INTIMATE CIRCLES OF CARING 143

    Thank You for Choosing Me 144

    Who Do You Belong To? 148

    The "Doing" of Intimacy 153

    Having a Close Circle of Intimates 157

    Seeing Intimacy through the Eyes of Intimacy 162

    Hearing Love from My Gran 165

    Mystery and Intimacy 170

    Intimacy as Life's Agenda 175

A Harlem Christmas Memory 178
A Love Letter to Kendi 184

PART FIVE 190
  SEXUALITY AND DISABILITY 190
    Learning to Be Sexy on One Leg 191
    Chair Dancing and the "Big Boss Turn" 194
    At 65: Snaggin' the Swagga of Spring 197
    Sexuality and Disability 201
    Love, Sex, and Disability: The Pleasures of Care 204

PART SIX 207
  THE DIY BOUDOIR 207
    The Body as Boudoir 208
    The Bed as Boudoir 213
    The Bath as Boudoir 217
    The Brain as Boudoir 221
    The Belly as Boudoir 225
    The Balm of Touch as Boudoir 229

PART SEVEN 232
  INTIMACY WITH OURSELVES 232
    Exhibit Yourself Beautifully to Yourself 233
    I Want to be Like Her When I'm Her Age 238
    Born to Be Intimate 241
    What Makes an Older Woman Sexy? 244
    My Wise Boudoir Birthday 247
    With Whom are You Intimate? 250
    Self-Care? Care! 253
    Intimacy and Vulnerability 259
    Yes, I Do Have Feelings about That 261
    Are We Having Fun Yet? 263

    Finding the Butterfly Inside 268
EPILOGUE 272

FORWARD

Into a world that often overlooks the extraordinary depths of love and intimacy in older adults, The Wise Boudoir emerges as a beacon of light, illuminating the path to a passionate and fulfilling connection. In this remarkable book, my dearest friend, Liv, embarks on a heartfelt exploration of love and intimacy that transcends age, revealing the beauty and wisdom that lie within the embrace of time.

Our society tends to emphasize the bloom of youth, leaving the rich tapestry of experiences and emotions that come with age overshadowed and underappreciated. But within the pages of this remarkable work, Liv crafts a narrative that celebrates the enduring power of sex, love, and the profound significance of intimacy for those of us who have journeyed through the seasons of life.

The Wise Boudoir invites us to witness the lives of extraordinary individuals who have gracefully matured, their spirits vibrant with wisdom, their hearts brimming with the fires of desire. Through poignant stories, shared experiences, and heartfelt reflections, Liv weaves a tapestry of narratives that shatter stereotypes and challenge societal norms, reminding us that love, sex and passion know no boundaries, no matter how many years we have accumulated.

With deep empathy and sensitivity, Liv guides us through the intricacies of older love, gently dismantling misconceptions and prejudices that may have clouded our perceptions. Drawing from a wealth of research, personal anecdotes, and conversations with those of us who have walked this path, The Wise Boudoir is a testament to Liv's unwavering commitment to enlightening hearts and minds.

This book is not only a celebration of love but a profound affirmation that intimacy can flourish and evolve at any age. Liv's eloquent prose captures the essence of these profound connections, reminding us that the pursuit of love, tenderness, and emotional fulfillment is a lifelong journey—a journey that grows more nuanced, more treasured with the passage of time.

The Wise Boudoir is an invaluable resource for individuals seeking to navigate the intricacies of love and intimacy in the later stages of life. Liv's compassionate guidance offers practical insights, gentle wisdom, and an unwavering belief in the transformative power of human connection.

As you embark on this passionate journey, may The Wise Boudoir be your guiding light, empowering you to embrace the boundless beauty of love and intimacy. May it remind you that the years which grace our lives bring not only wrinkles and silvered hair but also, an unparalleled depth of understanding, a capacity for compassion, and a reservoir of love waiting to be shared.

I am honored to introduce Liv's profound work to the world, a book that will undoubtedly touch the hearts of countless readers, transforming the way we perceive love, sex and intimacy, and the extraordinary beauty that unfolds when age meets desire.

With utmost admiration for Liv's courage, compassion, and unwavering dedication to uplifting others, I invite you to embark on this passionate journey of love and intimacy—a journey that will undoubtedly leave an indelible mark on your heart and soul.

Dr. Carole Stephens

INTRODUCTION

Social distancing was a new concept for me. Like most people, I first heard the term in early 2020 at the beginning of the COVID-19 pandemic. Public health officials explained that the deadly, highly infectious "novel" coronavirus was new to humans, and that our species had not yet built up "herd immunity" to it as we had to previous viruses like the flu and the common cold. They said that a special vaccine would have to be developed to help us survive the contagion, and that, until such a vaccine was available, *social distancing*, regular mask wearing, and frequent hand washing would be essential to slowing the virus's spread.

Little did we know, during the early months of 2020, that we'd be observing these virus- mitigation practices all year and would still be doing so when a couple of pharmaceutical companies introduced vaccines just before Christmas. And little did we know that the travel restrictions, lockdowns, quarantines, and local regulations imposed on us for months would so deeply affect our human need for intimacy, closeness, and touch.

By summer, long-form articles were appearing in national newspapers and magazines about how the isolation was psychologically harming people. Many who were used to regular, face-to-face contact with family, friends, neighbors, co-workers, fellow churchgoers, team mates, sexual partners and other "significant others" were feeling the separateness in ways that were emotionally painful. The relentless social isolation that virus mitigation mandated was causing mental health issues that required treatment, professional help and/or medication. And more, the prohibitions imposed by the pandemic were adding fuel to what had already been identified by health care providers as a "loneliness epidemic."

For many older adults, though, the loneliness was not new.

Older adults had been living with loneliness a long time. Before the pandemic, I'd completed a draft of this book as a compilation of the blogposts about intimacy for older adults that I'd written for The Wise Boudoir website. About a decade ago, I'd begun writing these blogs because I'd read the predictions that, as a result of advances in medicine, my generation of baby-boomers would be facing the prospect of longer life expectancy. Some experts said that we could easily add another 30 years to our lives. With longer lives, I reasoned, we'd also be facing unanswered questions about how to preserve intimacy and intimate relationships in late life.

Some of the big, unanswered question for me were these: Will we have a rich enough imagination to craft a fresh approach to intimacy in late life? Is our generation destined to become the vanguard for a demand for meaningful intimacy in older adulthood? How will the baby-boomer generation shape expectations among older adults as we model what life can look like at 100?

I've been thinking about intimacy a long time and wrote about the challenges of sexual intimacy a while ago in an essay, "If You Let Me Make Love to You, Then Why Can't I Touch Your Hair?" that appeared in an anthology about black women and our hair -- *Tenderheaded: A Comb-Bending Collection of Hair Stories* (Simon & Schuster, 2001). The essay is a sassy dramatization of the strategies some women concoct to maintain their fresh-from-the-salon hairdo while they have fun between-the-sheets. It's a piece with lots of laughs, and, in it, I play with the idea that, for some

INTRODUCTION

women, looking good during sex is more important than enjoying intimacy with a lover. A provocative idea, right?

I had not yet turned 60 when I wrote the piece, so my perspective did not contemplate the world I now inhabit. I'm close to 70 now and was diagnosed with multiple sclerosis a few years ago. My decade-long sweetie is a 71-year-old stroke survivor. He uses a cane to get around, and I use a rolling walker. Together, we embody some of the issues at play in the intimate lives of older adults. The prospect of longer life expectancy means that Eric and I will want to look good for each other as long as we can, and that our health will become a domain for our intimacy, too.

The Wise Boudoir is a collection of memoir-style essays on intimacy and relationship written through the eyes of a black woman from the baby-boom generation. It draws on my years as a blogger about intimacy in the lives of older adults and my experiences as a discussion leader for multi-racial women's groups. It introduces thought leaders who write about the importance of intimate relationships throughout the lifespan and explores the diverse ways we older adults are expressing intimacy today. And it asks some of the same questions I ask here.

The book is divided into sections that reflect the wide range of *intimacies* we baby-boomers marched through on the road to mature adulthood: The first section, "Dating, Mating, and Partnering after 50," glimpses the many ways we're connecting with our sweeties in later life. "Sex After 50" challenges us to look at how older adulthood has changed the way we think about sex. "A Look in the Rearview Mirror" takes us back to the years when early baby-boomers tackled the changes in sexual behavior that burst onto the scene in the 1960s. "Our Intimate Circles of Caring" honors the non-sexual intimacies we enjoy with family, friends and others close to us. "Sexuality and Disability" peeks into a world we know little about as outsiders, but one we'll learn

INTRODUCTION

more about as we grow older. "The DIY Boudoir" is a tour through the countless ways we can pleasure ourselves and our partners with the delicious sensations that are already alive in our bodies. And "Intimacy with Ourselves" zooms in on our inner lives and calls upon us to love and care for ourselves with the same committed attentiveness we'd offer a lover.

Why call this collection *The Wise Boudoir?* Well, if age and experience help us to gain wisdom, then 50 years of living has taught us a thing or two about intimacy. We've learned that we have a capacity for it that may have escaped us when we were younger, and that we have intimacy needs today that weren't even on our radar screen back then.

And as for the word, *boudoir?* It derives from the French verb, *bouder*, which means to brood or pout, and commonly refers to a woman's bedroom, or private sitting room. A boudoir, then, is a place where we can be intimate with our deepest desires, indulge our moods and *feel our feelings*. Indeed, it is from the renewal and refreshment we generate in our boudoir that we are better able to be intimate with others.

A wise boudoir, in the end, is a personal space where people on the far side of 50 can take stock of -- and ownership of -- their intimate lives.

It shouldn't surprise any of us over 50, then, that the pandemic's strictures did little to diminish our yearning for intimacy. Rather, the pause it imposed on our usual routines gave us a window into seeing how deeply we want and need our intimate relationships. And more, it showed us how important it is for us to give generous attention to the care and feeding of our "intimate self" if we want to enjoy the full flourishing of our well-being.

INTRODUCTION

That said, *The Wise Boudoir* now invites you to curl up with your favorite drink, get comfortable and feast on the stories about intimacy that are waiting for you inside.

Liv Wright
New York City

PART ONE

DATING, MATING, AND PARTNERING AFTER 50

PART ONE

Mature Marriage: Mandela and Machel

It was with great fascination that I read in July 1998 about Nelson Mandela and Graça Simbine Machel getting married on his 80th birthday. Graça was 52, and Mandela was 27 years older than she was. He was the first black president of post-apartheid South Africa, and she was the widow of Samora Machel, the first president of post-colonial Mozambique. Their marriage gave me hope that a deep love connection was possible at any age.

My parents separated when I was 5, so I didn't get to see them as a couple when I was growing up. I didn't have a clue, when I was dating as a young single, what a day-to-day marriage looked like. I certainly didn't know what to look for in a husband, and such ignorance might explain my three, short-lived engagements. My parents' post-marital experience didn't help, either. Neither ever had a "special other" after they divorced, and neither remarried.

In my mid-forties, I began paying attention to older couples who were in their second or third marriage (Graça was Mandela's third wife) and saw glimmers of what might be possible for me as a never-married wannabe. I still had not given up on the idea of getting married, but knew I'd have to "update" my ideas about marriage for the stage of life I was entering.

So, when Mandela and Machel married, I wanted to learn as much as I could about their mature marriage. The world knew about the upheavals in South Africa, and I had some previous knowledge of Mozambique. During the months that preceded the country's June 1975 independence from Portugal, I was living in southern Africa with my then-significant-other, Ed, an Irish-Catholic, Brooklyn-born political journalist. It was still the time of the Cold War, and he was covering the anti-colonial struggles in Angola, Southwest Africa, Rhodesia, and Mozambique against the backdrop of US-Soviet relations.

Mozambique was very much on my radar screen. One of the founders and the first president of Mozambique's anti-colonial, liberation movement, *Frente de Liberaçäo de Moçambique,* or FRELIMO, was Eduardo Mondlane, an anthropologist who earned his Ph.D. at Northwestern University, and who had been a visiting professor there in 1967 when I, as a sophomore, took one of his classes. He taught his students about the independence movements that were then sweeping southern Africa and helped us understand the continent's anti-colonial struggles. He also mentored and befriended us black students, knowing that we'd only been admitted to the mostly white school in large numbers the previous year. From his time as a student, he knew that there had been very few American blacks on campus, and wanted to do as much as he could to help us.

For years after attending his class, I closely followed the politics of FRELIMO and Mozambique. During the late 1960s, Mondlane and other FRELIMO principals, including Samora Machel lived in Dar es Salam, Tanzania, where the officially banned organization was headquartered. It was as a freedom-fighter living there that Dr. Mondlane was killed by a Lisbon-orchestrated parcel bomb in February 1969, and would never see his country's independence. After Mondlane's assassination, Machel became the head of FRELIMO and distinguished himself as one of the most respected guerilla commanders in the anti-colonial effort.

In 1974, the political party in Lisbon that had been fighting the long colonial war was voted out of office, and Portuguese troops left Mozambique. Samora Machel became president of the independent country in June 1975, and married Graça Simbine in September of that year.

Twelve years younger than President Machel, Graça was an accomplished First Lady: She had graduated from Lisbon University with a concentration in modern languages, earned a law degree, taught in FRELIMO schools, and been trained to strip an assault rifle as a guerilla fighter. In her husband's administration, she served as Minister of Culture and Education, cutting in half the illiteracy rate of Mozambique's school children during her tenure.

In 1986, President Machel died in a mysterious plane crash on the mountainous border between Mozambique and South Africa. Graça would forever believe that her husband had been killed by the South African government, politically threatened by an independent, black-ruled, socialist country on its border. While she was in mourning for Samora, both Mandelas wrote to her. Nelson had been in prison for more than 20 years. Winnie was under house arrest. Both understood her grief.

Nelson and Graça became friends after his release from prison and subsequent divorce from Winnie. At first, they met casually at public events in the early 1990s but grew much closer when Mandela became surrogate father – in the African tradition – to the late President Machel's six children -- the two youngest were born to President Machel and Graça. It was a role Mandela assumed after the fatal stroke in 1993 of the siblings' previous surrogate father, Oliver Tambo, the ANC President who had been President Machel's lifelong friend as well as Mandela's former law partner and political comrade.

Nelson and Graça's relationship blossomed into something deeper, and he – according to his memoir – ardently pursued her hand in marriage. The long walk of Nelson Mandela had seen him as revolutionary, commander, fugitive, prisoner, president, and icon. These are lonely places for a person to live, and Graça Machel understood those places.

"We were both very, very lonely," she once said. "We both wanted someone you could talk to, someone who'd understand."

Mandela and Machel are serious people. Those whose lives are shaped by physical or psychic terrorism become serious people. To be shaped by apartheid, colonialism, Jim Crow, genocide, or war is to be made serious. As human beings, though, there is always the part of us that longs to be renewed. With renewal, anything is possible, and maybe that's what mature marriage offers: renewal in the eyes of that Special Other.

After his marriage to Graça, Mandela wrote:

I cannot describe my joy and happiness to receive the love and warmth of such a humble, but gracious and brilliant lady. It gives me unbelievable comfort and satisfaction to know that there [is] somebody somewhere in the universe on whom I can rely, especially on matters where my political comrades cannot provide me.

And in a TV interview, he said:

I'm in love with a lovely lady. I don't regret the reverses and setbacks because late in my life I'm blooming like a flower because of the love and support she's given me.

I've seen several of Machel's TV interviews, and heard her speak about the renewal that Mandela brought into her life:

The beginning of our closeness was two people who had been very hurt by life. It would take somebody like Madiba to help me live again, and to believe that love was possible.

And I was especially inspired by what she told CNN in 2008:

We met in life at a time when we were both settled. We were grown up. We were settled. We knew the value of a companion, of a partner. Because of that, we have enjoyed this relationship in a really special way. It's not like

PART ONE

when you are still young, you are too demanding. No, no. We just accept each other as we are. And we enjoy every single day as if it is the last day.

I can appreciate now how much I needed to hear from "the elders" on the subject of love and marriage. Like other baby-boomers, I read the pulp published for my generation, and knew it wasn't as rich as I wanted it to be. It wasn't *elder wisdom*.

Elder wisdom embodies humility, maturity, life experience, *failure,* dignity, grace -- and peace with one's mortality. People knew that elder wisdom was present when they were with Nelson Mandela and Graça Machel.

Thank you, Nelson and Graça, for your mature marriage, and thank you for passing your elder wisdom to us.

PART ONE

Whose Couch is Gonna Be Thrown Out?

Here's a story about a mature couple that gets married and decides not to live together.

I had a long chat a few weeks ago with one of my divorced friends from college whom I hadn't spoken with in more than a decade. A Chicago native, she told me that when she remarried, she and her new husband decided to continue living in their own homes. Intrigued by the idea, I asked for permission to share her story. I had written about the idea of separate homes for married couples in my blog but had not yet spoken to someone who was doing it.

"He loves his condo and I love my garden," she said simply. "He's a city guy whose apartment is walking distance from the lake and convenient to downtown restaurants, galleries, and outdoor jazz in the summer. And I'm a suburbanite."

My friend is a visual artist who retired from teaching art to high school students. A large portion of her house is dedicated to an art studio where she still paints every day. When we spoke, she was preparing for an upcoming exhibit that will feature her work.

"It was a tough decision," she said. "My husband and I don't like the same things, and I knew I didn't want to spend time arguing with him about color, furniture or whose couch was gonna be thrown out. So, we decided to keep our own places."

Both he and she have modest pensions from Chicago's Board of Education and live comfortably. They manage their money separately, and when they go out for dinner or on trips, they go Dutch treat.

PART ONE

"I'm pretty low maintenance," she explained. "I scrimped and saved to buy my house and spent years getting the garden to be just the way I like it. I'm happy with what I have, and last year, told my husband not to give me any more presents. I have all the necklaces, bracelets, and earrings I could ever wear."

My friend also told me that when she and her husband first talked about where they might live, she sensed that he was uncomfortable with the idea of giving up his condo. He had been married for nearly 30 years and bought the new condo after his divorce. He was 60 and it was his first apartment.

"He absolutely loves it," she said. "I don't."

What she does love, though, is what being married has meant in her life.

"We're two people devoted to helping each other and every day is better than the day before. As little things come up, you think about the other person and what would make them happy."

For this couple, no one's "couch" was thrown out.

But if "couch" can be seen as a metaphor for comfort, then his condo and her garden are exactly that. Success in our relationships as older adults means preserving our measures of comfort. We're happier when we're comfortable.

As I think about it, my circumstances are not that different from my friend's. I'm very comfortable where I live, too. I've been here a long time and have built a strong network of support. It wouldn't be easy for me to leave either.

The term sociologists use for people in relationships like my friend's is LAT or *Living Apart Together*. The term describes couples who have a long-term, intimate relationship, but have chosen to live separately. LAT relationships are growing among older adults and include single people like me as well as married couples. LATs include the rich and famous and, increasingly, the not-so-rich and not-so-famous. My 90-something uncle and his 80-something sweetheart, for example, were a LAT couple for nearly 50 years. They now live together because he'd rather be with her than in the "facility" his adult children were considering for him.

I saw a segment about LATs on You Tube, and one expert raised the question of whether such couples have the same degree of bonding as couples who live together. She felt that the compromises and accommodations made by married cohabiters help them to bond more deeply.

The controversy will continue as the number of LAT relationships grows. Indeed, such living arrangements are increasing at a time when baby-boomers are sorting out the kinds of relationships we'll want to have as older adults.

My friend used an expression that captured my heart when we spoke. She said that with her husband she had found "a complete resting place." I knew she wasn't talking about a physical place, but rather the caring space that she and her husband have created for each other.

Don't tell anyone, but I think that's where they really live.

PART ONE

The Magic Mirror – Our Lovers, Ourselves

Last weekend, I went to a performance of *Cougar: The Musical* and laughed until I cried. Written by Donna Moore, a gifted playwright, lyricist and composer, the cabaret-style show tells the story of three women over 40 who have their sights fixed on finding hot young men to be their lovers. At the end of the play, one character starts dating a man her own age who brings new excitement into her life; one finds a younger man who is perfect for her; and one discovers a deeper relationship with herself.

According to an AARP survey, some 34 percent of women over 40 are dating younger men. The phenomenon of the *Cougar* has been around for a long time, and such Hollywood stars as Madonna and Susan Sarandon are notable *femmes fatales* in the category. My favorite old-school Cougar story, though, is that of Elizabeth Taylor and her seventh husband (she married Richard Burton twice), Larry Fortensky.

Taylor and Fortensky met in the late 1980s when they were both in rehab at the Betty Ford Center. When they married in 1991, she was 59 and he was 39. By 1996, they were divorced, but remained good friends. In an interview after Taylor's death in 2011, one of Fortensky's close relatives was quoted as saying that the marriage ended because he (Fortensky) "didn't want to be *Mr. Elizabeth Taylor* anymore."

Unlike Liz and Larry, all Cougar relationships aren't doomed. For example, Lily, one of the characters in *Cougar*, is a recent divorcée who meets a younger man during the course of the play. He's a New York actor who majored in theater at NYU, and she had been a working actress before she got married. They share a lot of interests and hit it off right away. They fall in love but decide not to share a future together. They are mature enough to see that their life paths are headed in different directions. And before their mutual decision to go separate ways, Lily affirms in song that, unlike the husband she divorced, the younger guy "gets" her.

Also in a successful Cougar relationship is my widowed friend from college who met a man 15 years her junior and moved with him to a small college town in upstate New York. There, they bought an old-school general store and started a bed and breakfast business. When our group of college friends saw her at our class reunion last year, she looked younger than we'd ever seen her. She and her husband are a *poster couple* for the kind of relationship Cougars can have with younger men.

For a Cougar, having a relationship with a younger man definitely has an impact on how she looks and feels. So says the self-proclaimed Cougar, Valerie Gibson, author of two books on the subject: (1) *Cougar: A Guide for Older Women Dating Younger Men*, and (2) *Younger Men: How to Find Them, Date Them, Mate Them*, and Marry Them. She says that having a youthful person on your arm makes you feel good, desirable, and ageless.

France Schott-Billmann, a French dance historian and psychoanalyst, agrees with Gibson, and offers an additional explanation: She says the fact that a Cougar might look ten years younger and that her boyfriend might seem more mature can be explained by a phenomenon she calls the *Magic Mirror – in which the way another person sees you defines you.*

It's not hard to see how the Magic Mirror works. Whether you're Elizabeth Taylor, the fictional divorcée, or my college friend, when your young lover lusts for you, rockets of life-enhancing hormones sweep over your body and trigger sensations that are different from those you experience with a man your age. You're young again, and you're desirable!

The Magic Mirror works both ways, though. A similar magic happens for the young man.

In Cougar culture, they are called *Cubs,* and it can be heady stuff for them, too. In their book, *Older Women, Younger Men: New Options for Love and Romance,* authors Felicia Brings and Susan Winter talk about the advantages that mature women reflect back to younger men.

Here are some quotes from their book that were excerpted in an article posted on the erstwhile *iVillage.*com:

They (older women) were able to see things in me that I could not see in myself. Also, there were levels of honesty unlike anything I've experienced even with best friends.

I take better care of myself now. She is a best friend who reflects back to me what a good person I am, which builds my confidence and self-esteem.

I grew up a lot with her. Yeah, definitely, she helped me to grow up. She made me realize how important I could be in making someone else happy.

I have a preference for women starting at about 10 years older than myself and up. It's adventurous for both of us because it's a whole new exciting journey. Younger women just don't allow me to grow in the ways older women do.

The Magic Mirror effect is not just for Cougar-Cub couples. It has been very much at play in my relationship with Eric, and we are both in our sixties. I'm sure that I'd be feeling differently about my MS diagnosis if I didn't have someone in my life who sees me as lusty, funny, feminine, and pretty. I met Eric six months after he survived a stroke in which he lost the use of his right arm. Then, as now, I see him as sexy, funny, manly, and handsome.

When I read those quotes from the young men, I could see that their experiences are similar to the way the Magic Mirror works in my relationship. Eric has seen things in me that I could not see in myself; made me realize how important I could be in making someone else happy; and helped me to grow.

The first thing he asked me to do when we got together was to help him restore some of the cognitive capacity he lost with the stroke. It was an unusual request, but he believed that an intimate relationship would demand more of him mentally than any therapy his doctors might prescribe. He was right. In the Magic Mirror of our relationship, he grew stronger and more productive as an artist than either he or I could have imagined.

Without a doubt, the Magic Mirror has been our friend. When we gaze into it, we see the way he sees me and the way I see him.

In the boudoir of our relationship, the Magic Mirror holds a place of honor.

PART ONE

Sadie Hawkins 2.0

Leap Year only comes every four years, but for some reason, I'm thinking today about February 29. I've always thought of it as Sadie Hawkins Day, a day when women can ask men to go out on a date. As it turns out, I was all wrong about February 29, so I looked up Sadie Hawkins online. To my surprise, I learned that the Sadie Hawkins phenomenon started with *L'il Abner,* one of the comic strips that war-babies and baby-boomers grew up with. Its creator, Al Capp, first created the Sadie Hawkins character in November 1937. Back then, young women were expected to marry by their early twenties and were officially spinsters at 35.

According to the strip, Sadie Hawkins's father, one of the founders of the rural town of Dogpatch, the setting for the newspaper strip, was frantic that his unattractive, 35-year-old, never-married daughter, Sadie, was still living at home. So, he decreed a foot race in which his daughter would run after the town's eligible bachelors until she caught one. The one she caught would become her husband. The other unmarried women in Dogpatch liked the idea so much that Sadie Hawkins Day became an annual event in the town every November. If a woman caught a bachelor and dragged him across the finish line before sundown (usually kicking and screaming), he had to "marry up" with her according to Dogpatch law.

Outside the strip, Sadie Hawkins Day gained traction in the popular culture. By the early 1940s, the comic strip event had swept the nation and acquired a life of its own. It especially captured the imagination of young people in high schools and colleges who turned the gender role-reversal activity into Sadie

Hawkins dances. Such dances were events where -- instead of waiting to be asked -- girls and young women could invite boys and young men to be their dates.

By 1952, Sadie Hawkins Day had become a national day-long, pseudo-holiday typically observed on the second Saturday in November.

So, where did I get the idea that Sadie Hawkins Day was February 29?

Well, it seems there really were folk traditions around the world that permitted a woman to propose marriage during leap year, or more restrictively, on leap day, February 29. But unlike in Dogpatch, the man of her choice could refuse her proposal and materially compensate her in accordance with local rules and traditions. That's how I got it all mixed up.

I was thinking about Sadie Hawkins Day because of a conversation I had with a sex therapist friend of mine. She reminded me that women over 50 face a mounting "gender disparity" as we get older. Simply put, there are fewer and fewer men to do things with. Demographers hold that the natural sex ratio for babies at birth is 1.06 male/female, or slightly more boys than girls. The ratio decreases as the age of men and women increases, and among older adults there are many more women than there are men.

Statistically, women have a higher life expectancy than men. Men historically have a higher death rate because of such natural causes as heart attacks and strokes, and such violent causes as homicides, accidents, and war. According to the US Census, among adults aged 50 and older, there are approximately 7 men for every 10 women.

And let's not even talk about the older men who are healthy enough to be targeted by latter-day Sadie Hawkinses. My father passed away at the age of 99, having had no chronic health

PART ONE

issues and being free of taking any daily medications. He was a pretty healthy guy well into his 90s and was the object of much attention among the ladies at his church. They all predeceased him, to be sure, but while they were still prowling around, Daddy had a target on his back!

There is also the Sadie Hawkins story my friend, a real estate developer, told me about the assisted living facility his partner built. To the amazement of staff at the facility, at least three women would visit every new guy on the day he moved in to check him out and size him up.

The sex therapist hears about gender disparity in most of the age groups she treats, and women of all ages are exploring alternatives to the traditions they were born into. In her practice, older women are engaged in mate sharing, selecting other women as partners, and developing dormant masturbation skills to keep pleasure alive.

Sadie Hawkins 2.0 is one of the strategies we baby-boomer women can use to address the demographic fact that there are simply more of us at this age than there are fellas.

PART ONE

Money and the Baby-Boomer Boudoir

Newsflash: It looks like women are going to become the primary breadwinner in most households in our lifetime. And the trend seems to be happening worldwide! What effect will this shift have on sexual behaviors in the bedroom, and how will couples adjust to it?

I just finished reading *The Richer Sex: How the New Majority of Female Breadwinners is Transforming Sex, Love and Families* by Liza Mundy. In it, Mundy reports on the voluminous social research that's examining this sea change in male-female relationships.

It seems that women are earning more college degrees than men, and are also outnumbering men in medical, law and business school enrollments. Fewer than half of all adults aged 21 to 64 in the U.S. today are married, and more than half of all babies are born to single mothers. The number of households in which the woman goes to work, and the man stays home to take care of the kids continues to grow.

Today, only a very small percent of male earners has the ability to support a family on just one income.

The sea change will largely affect people who are younger than us baby-boomers, though. Our generation still seems hardwired to the images we saw on TV in the 1950s and 1960s. Women still want guys to do the heavy lifting in the area of income, and guys still want women in secondary roles. Our generation will learn a profound lesson when we see that the old paradigm wasn't carved in stone.

When I was on the phone the other day with one of my divorced girlfriends, for example, she was sizing up the single male retirees in her social circle and calculating in her head their annual pensions. She was trying to decide which ones were worthy of her time.

"I don't want to be a nurse with a purse," she explained.

To be sure, the era of the large, guaranteed pension came to an end during the working lives of us baby-boomers. Consider that a General Motors car today has more of its production costs connected to health benefits for the company's retirees' than to steel. Consider, too, that the City of Detroit filed for bankruptcy because of its inability to pay pensions to the city's retirees.

Welcome to the *post-pension* world.

In the mid-1980s – when we baby-boomers were in our 30s and 40s -- the guaranteed, defined benefit pension began to go south, and the market-based, defined contribution, or 401(k), became the retirement plan most of us were offered.

I have a retired friend who had the good fortune to work for a trade association whose pension plan combined both the defined benefit pension *and* the 401(k). He is a rarity. He's secure and travels wherever he likes, whenever he likes. Only 10 percent of today's retirees still have guaranteed, or defined benefit, pensions.

To be sure, there is a 'sizing up' of assets that goes on among residents in retirement communities. Your fellow retirees want to know what you're bringing to the table. (Yes, there's a pecking order even among retired folks.)

When I was selling life insurance back in the 1970s (I've done some of everything.), the conventional retirement model was that of a three-legged stool. The first leg was your pension, the second was your Social Security income, and the third was your savings. Savings! Remember savings? And now pensions are on the ropes, too. Good grief!

So, how are we going to "feather the nest" in the baby-boomer boudoir? For one thing, we may have to abandon the man-on-top/woman-on-bottom archetype we grew accustomed to and avoid laying guilt trips on each other for not fulfilling traditional gender roles.

In her book, Mundy talks about how much we can learn from same-sex couples who aren't locked into traditional gender expectations.

That might be a good place for us to start.

In the same way that many older adults have learned to text and use such social media as Facebook, Instagram, and Twitter, we may have to learn from younger generations that there are alternative ways to feather a nest.

A while ago, I read that some of the largest corporations in the U.S. are assigning younger employees to mentor older employees on the use of their company's newest technology. It occurs to me that we baby-boomers can learn from younger adults about the gender thing, too.

Our generation was hardwired to the idea that men should have more money than women. Maybe the time has come for us to throw that idea overboard.

PART ONE

Our Gin Game

I saw the play, *The Gin Game,* on Broadway in 1978 during the season it debuted, received a Tony nomination for Best Play and won the Pulitzer Prize for Drama. Since then, it's been produced on six continents and translated into dozens of languages. I wanted to see what the celebrated two-character drama about older adults had to say about intimacy in later life, so I recently watched a filmed version of it on You Tube.

The video was a filmed version of the inaugural Broadway production that I'd seen. It starred Jessica Tandy (she won a Tony Award for Best Actress for her performance), and Hume Cronyn was her co-star. Often called the "premier theater couple," Tandy and Cronyn are known for having created a distinguished body of work together. When I saw them in *The Gin Game,* they had been married for 35 years and had played opposite each other in scores of venues. The mastery they brought to their performances as Fonsia (Tandy) and Weller (Cronyn), two residents in a nursing home, was matched only by the intimacy of two creatives who know each other as well as you can know another person.

In the play, Fonsia and Weller strike up an acquaintance in the nursing home's day room and learn to enjoy each other's company. Fonsia accepts Weller's offer to teach her how to play gin rummy, and then wins every hand after he has taught her. Weller doesn't like losing to Fonsia and becomes increasingly frustrated with each loss.

During the card games, the two have long conversations in which they become both closer and more hostile. They divulge what their chronic illnesses are and what their life aspirations were when they were younger. They reveal that they used to like to dance, that their relationships with their families are frayed and that they are now living on welfare. As their mutual hostility mounts, they try more and more to expose each other's weaknesses and humiliate one another.

According to playwright, D. J. Coburn, *The Gin Game* is about two people who are nearing the end of their lives with many essential areas of the life experience unexamined and never confronted. The card game, he says, "draws both characters into a virtual death-spiral of revelation that reaches to the core of their beings."

I thought I knew the play well until I went to the playwright's website and read his notes about the play. It was there that I learned about the *scorecard*. The website is where the author tells us that the Fonsia and Weller gin rummy scorecard drives the whole play. Coburn tells us that, as an artistic consultant to two major revivals, he discovered that his actors neither knew how to play gin rummy, nor how "Hollywood" scoring (as insisted upon by the Weller character) works.

Significantly, the actors in the revivals did not know that the energy needed for each scene is generated by the game's scorecard as written in the play. (Coburn eventually posted the scorecard for each scene at his website so that performers in subsequent productions can see it.) I've seen the play several times and never paid attention to the score either. I assumed that references to it were just "stage business." But scoring -- I now know -- is at the heart of the play.

Ah, scoring.

I began to think about scoring in the "gin game" we all play – the game of life. As we get older, we keep score about a whole lot of things: our monthly income; the accomplishments of our adult children and grandchildren, looking young, managing

PART ONE

our weight, dental woes, knee and joint pain, pensions, surgeries, and more.

Some of us even rule out potential intimates because their scores are too low. To be sure, online dating sites are all about scoring, and the metrics we use at such sites are all about the mating marketplace. We compare matches and apply scores to them. "I can do better," we tell ourselves.

We also *score* our spouses and significant others and tell ourselves that we could do better in life if we had a different partner. Better than what, I always ask. Our intimates are our mirrors, and they are in our lives for a reason. They might reflect parts of ourselves we don't like, but changing the mirror won't change what's being reflected.

So, in the end, what is *The Gin Game* telling us? The message at the playwright's website is clear: *it's never too late to engage the essential parts of ourselves that are still unexamined or were never confronted.*

Who is the person, or who are the persons who will trigger such self-examination? Who will confront our unexamined parts? Will we meet them in the nursing home day room, on match dot com, or do we already know them?

Maybe it will be through our intimates, or through intimacy itself, that we will finally reveal ourselves to ourselves, and have a chance to win at the game of life.

When such intimacy presents itself, though, will we be open to it?

PART ONE

Because with Him I Feel All "Girly"

The other day, I was complaining on the phone to one of my girlfriends about Eric, my boyfriend for the past 10 years. She challenged me and said that I must be getting something of value from the relationship if I'm still with him.

"What *are* you getting?" she asked as a long-time friend would.

I thought for a moment, then said, "Well, for sure, I'm getting a lot, but what comes to mind right now is that with him I get to feel *girly*. It's a side of me that I've neglected, and I want more of it in my life."

"Okay, so what do you mean by girly?" she asked, coaxing me to say more.

Again, I had to think. I told her that for me girly conjured up such words as flirtatious, giggly and *blushy*. Girly is how I felt 50 years ago when some alpha male athlete swaggered into the school cafeteria, sidled up to the table where I was sitting with my friends and said, "hello." The rush of hormones that goes on among teenagers with the simple word, *hello,* is one of life's mysteries. That's what I mean when I say *girly*.

I'm post-menopausal now, and the notion of girly is not associated with women my age. Baby-making is behind us, and so are the juices that compelled us to want to make babies. We have raised children (and grandchildren, in some cases), worked on our jobs for decades and taken care of elders. Girly might not describe us now, but we haven't forgotten what it feels like.

Eric brought the word back into my vocabulary when I met him. He and I went to high school here in New York City during the 1960s and had been "lunch room lizards" at our respective schools. We knew about the flirtations that went on between, say, athletes and cheerleaders, and we've talked often about high school hierarchies and cliques. It was he who reminded me of the phenomenon of *girly*.

I had forgotten that guys were the target of our girly ways, but Eric hadn't. He had been stung by a few pretty girls at his school who wanted to be "just friends." He knew about the whole girly thing from a different perspective and noticed that I had been doing girly things with him in our relationship. He recalled that mine were the same behaviors he had seen years before when he was a young man.

Young women today seem to be all over the map about the girly thing. When I went online to see what they were saying, I read that being girly for many of them is associated with spending lots of time and money on hair, nails, make-up, and clothes. I learned that, conversely, some young women don't want to spend their time fussing with their appearance like that and would rather put on a pair of jeans and a T-shirt and call it a day.

Running in the background for us baby-boomer women, though, is that disapproving look from our mothers, and the less-than-subtle question: *You're not going out looking like THAT, are you?* My mother, for example, who passed away when she was 85, wouldn't think of leaving the house without putting on her lipstick. And when she and I took her ailing sister to the emergency room for what would prove to be a terminal illness, my aunt insisted that we fetch her handbag before leaving the apartment. In it, were her comb, face powder, lipstick, and nail file – some of the girly accoutrements that women our mothers' age always kept with them.

I want to embrace more of my girly side now. I'm from that generation of corporate women who read such books as *Games Mother Never Taught You,* and who learned that being girly at

PART ONE

work was a no-no. When I was a member of the New York chapter of the trade organization, Women in Cable, in the early 1980s, we produced a musical revue, for one of our fund raisers, in which I performed a parody song that I co-wrote with another member. The song was called "Masculinity," and it poked fun at the measures some women were taking to stay on the executive-career-track by not being too girly in the workplace. Here are some of the lyrics:

Masculinity, masculinity, you must get some of that in this one word is the epitome of the real bureaucrat.
Masculine style and masculine manners, masculine stuff to eat That's the requisite prerequisite of the executive suite.

Such was the message we women executives in the 1980s got before Mary Barra at General Motors; Ursula Burns at Xerox; and Ginni Rometty at IBM became CEOs of their respective companies. Back then, many of us neglected our girly side.

As an older woman, I want to connect with my girly side more and more.

When I spoke with my physical therapist about getting a walker on rollers to increase my mobility (my cane was proving insufficient for good balance), I thought about the girl inside me who still flirts, giggles, and blushes. She knows that she can fuss about her hair, nails, make-up, and clothes whether she moves around on a walker, wheelchair, cane, or stilettos.

She knows that girly is a state of mind that is not bound by age, the amount of gray hair she has, how many pounds she weighs, or the number of prescriptions she fills every month.

Girly is gifting we women are born with that will keep on giving -- if we let it.

A few months ago, Eric and I met a woman at a concert who was about to celebrate her 100th birthday. She flirted with him mercilessly and introduced him to others as her new boyfriend. Her hearing wasn't sharp enough to hear what Eric was saying to her, but she flirted her heart away and enjoyed every moment.

    I think I'll take a page out of her book and let the girl who still lives in me play to her heart's content and have as much fun as she wants to. I'll let her giggle with abandon and flirt without mercy, joyfully delighting in the incredible gift she will always be.

PART ONE

Flirt!

A few hours ago, I got a Facebook post that was headlined, *How to Stay Young & Hot Forever: Advice from a 96-Year-Old Grandma.* The hot grandma had some great tips, and they were right there in the article. Her granddaughter wrote the piece and lists "20 Ways to Stay Young and Hot from Someone Who Really Knew How."

My favorite was #8, *Flirt with Life.*

When I saw it, I was reminded of the women in their nineties who have flirted with Eric when he and I were out socially. I've written before that I want to be like them when I'm in my nineties. But the granddaughter makes a new distinction about her grandmother's flirting and writes of it this way:

Flirt with life—not just with men and women, but with all of what life has to offer. This will make you feel young, hopeful, and excited to get out of bed every day. My grandma enjoyed flirting with any man in uniform, and I am certain that if she were around today, she would flirt with my boyfriend while also flirting with the idea of buying new shoes.

Flirting with life is a new concept for me, but I get it. I get it that being open to new people, new places, and new experiences will freshen my outlook. I get it that being available to life will make me more interesting to others and bring new adventures into my life. I get it that when I'm in my nineties, I want to be a woman who's fun to be around.

I'm writing about a woman today who is a generation older than I am. Earlier this week, a woman I know who a generation is younger than I am learned that I was writing this blog and asked why I hadn't told her about it. I said that I was writing the blog for baby-boomer women and thought she

PART ONE

wouldn't share our concerns. She said that I was mistaken and that her early- forties friends are concerned about our issues, too.

Which brings me back to flirting. It doesn't matter how old we are; flirting is a lifelong activity. We may think of it narrowly as a part of romance, courtship, or dating. But it's broader than that. It's part of being human.

Some time ago, there was a TV commercial that featured two gray-hared, older women -- identical twins – who are shopping for a car. They flirt mercilessly with the young salesman during their test drive, and the twin sitting in the driver's seat touches his lips with a finger-kiss as they negotiate the price. Now, that's flirting!

Men even flirt with me when I'm using my walker. The other day, when I was exiting my local MacDonald's having just used the ladies' room there, a gentleman complimented me on my hair, helped me with the door, and asked why I was using the walker. When I told him I had MS, he looked sad and nodded understandingly. Later, our paths crossed again, and he stopped me to chat enthusiastically about an infomercial he'd seen about blenders that can grind up the healing foods that will cure me. I believe the gentleman was flirting with me!

Flirting is a life skill without which our lives would be duller, lonelier, and a lot less fun. So says Elizabeth Clark, the "Flirt Guru," in *Flirting for Dummies*. I picked up the book a few months ago because I wanted to know more about flirting, and how it might help me to be more playful. Clark is bold in her claims about the essential role of flirting in human life, and introduces her book this way:

If you could learn one skill to improve your self-confidence and your listening skills, help you meet more people and project the right impression, and show you how to read and react to body language, not only would you want to learn it, you'd probably expect it to be on the curriculum in every school. Unfortunately, it isn't because this particular skill is flirting, and it has bad press.

She says it has bad press because, in addition to making you friends and improving your relationships, people also use it to get dates, gain sexual advantage and seduce the unsuspecting. Whatever the case may be, flirting is a great life skill.

Clark asserts that flirting is a naturally inherent skill that was given to us by Mother Nature and that all we have to do is follow the major routes that have already been mapped into the human brain: Making eye contact, smiling, touching intentionally, and mirroring body language.

My take-away is that the "art" (can I call it that?) of flirting is like the art of conversing: It's one of those "forever" skills that we use to connect with others. And connecting with others is going to become more and more important as we get older. Being skilled at connecting can mean either good health or so-so health, experts say, and I want to learn all I can now about connecting. Indeed, I want to do everything I can to help my "forever" last as long as possible.

PART ONE

On Savoring and Being Savored

I first learned about the art of *savoring* when I saw Dr. Christine Northrup's PBS special, *Glorious Women Never Age*. Toward the end of the program, she talked about people who are thriving at the age of 100 and tells us that they're doing so because they are good at *savoring*.

Savoring? What's that, I thought.

I looked up the word and saw that *savoring* is the *use of thoughts or actions to increase the intensity, duration, and appreciation of positive experiences and emotions*. The lead researcher today on savoring is Fred Bryant, Ph.D., a social psychologist at Loyola University Chicago, who is seen as the father of the concept. The main idea of *savoring* is that by being mindfully engaged and aware of your feelings during positive events, you can increase happiness in both the short and long run.

Ah, happiness. Who wouldn't want more of that?

Bryant, the pied piper of savoring, proclaims that we can all learn how to be good at it. He wrote a book called *Savoring* with his colleague, Joseph Veroff, in which he discusses the many ways we can have savoring experiences: Music, nature, reading, having a great meal, visiting with friends.

When I picked up the book, I went straight to the section on sex and intimacy. I wanted to know what the author had to say about savoring and being savored by our sweethearts and rushed to read that part ASAP. (I felt the way we must have felt as kids when we knew where the "good stuff" was in one of our parents' books or magazines.)

The "redeeming" value of skipping ahead as an older adult is knowing that savoring and being savored by a sweetheart is good for our health and longevity. And to his credit, Bryant puts the health benefits of savoring right after the romance part. He writes the way professors do, unfortunately, so I had to do my best to put it all together in a tidy way. The good news is that Bryant gives us the story of Jack and Jill to make it easier:

… nothing so deeply conveys to Jill Jack's joy of loving her as when he communicates to her how much he savors the joy of having her in his life, and vice versa.

That's it! *To savor the joy of having my sweetheart in my life, and to be likewise savored.*

I want to savor and be savored like that, I thought.

Bryant tells us that a comparable good feeling occurs in a close friendship when one friend says to the other: "It doesn't get any better than this." I spoke with one of my close friends the other day about savoring, and she gave me the word she likes to use for hugging. She said that when she parts company with a loved one, she "rubs them up." I like that expression. I've been "rubbed up" by her before, and I've savored it immensely. It feels good.

The good news in the book is that we can all learn how to enhance and broaden our capacity to savor our loved ones, and to, in turn, be savored by them: We can laugh with them, hug them, reminisce about positive experiences shared with them, anticipate future good times with them, and express our love, appreciation and gratitude for their presence in our lives.

Bryant's research-academic word for such exchanges is *affirmation.* People savor the feeling of being affirmed for who they really are and enjoy feeling that they are important in your life. His long-term research with married couples who were interviewed during the first, third and seventh years of their marriages found that spouses who feel really affirmed by their partners have marriages that are strong and long-lasting.

PART ONE

And here's where the health effects come in: Savoring is good for our immune system.

Researchers call it a "protective factor" that we can build on every day by finding joy in everyday life. In so doing, we decrease our vulnerability to disease and maybe even lower our health-care costs. Over the course of a lifetime, a rich and varied history of savoring predicts not only a higher quality of life, but a higher quantity of life, too.

So, holy cow! That's what Dr. Northrup was talking about at the end of her PBS special. It's good to know that every day will bring opportunities to affirm the people I love, and to savor -- and be savored by -- them.

I think I'll savor that thought for a moment.

PART ONE

Are We Fighting About *That* Again?

Eric and I had a fight last week. And not surprisingly, it was a fight we've had many times before. We're like most couples that way. We argue over and over about the same stuff. I went online and looked up the top 10 reasons couples' fight. The topic seems to be standard fare for lifestyle magazines, so there were tons of articles on the subject.

There were the usual suspects, of course: Money, children, sex, housework, job issues, and in-laws. There were also some kinds of fights that look like they could be about one of the partners' on-going complaints but were part of a broader issue. Examples of these were fights about whether the cell phone should come to the dinner table (or to bed), or who gets to hold the remote-control device when the couple watches TV, or with whose family the couple will spend the holidays.

For those of us over 50, there is also a category of fighting that a person "ages" into. It's the category called "old hurts," and, if you live long enough, or have been with your partner long enough, there'll be a truckload of those to fight about. That's what Eric and I were fighting about.

I wanted to take a serious look at the issue of couples fighting about these old hurts and see why couples rehash things the way they do. I'm not that different from other people, so I thought that what I'd discover in my search might be helpful to others. My direction turned out to be a false start, though. It seems that couples aren't fighting about what we think we're fighting about at all. So, why *are* we fighting?

According to psychologists and brain scientists, we can't help it. It's in our DNA. The human brain has evolved to need social connection for its survival, and we human beings get anxious and fearful -- and want to fight -- when we feel that our *connection* to those we love and care about is being threatened.

"Lovers fight," says psychotherapist Dr. Steven Stosny, "when they believe their partners don't care about how they feel. They're mostly fighting about the pain of disconnection."

I get it now. I get it about the cell phone at dinner. Indeed, the fight I had with Eric last week was about our not being able to connect. I wasn't free to talk when he wanted to tell me something that was very important to him. I needed to sleep, and he needed to talk. Both of us felt that the other didn't care about how we felt. Having someone special in my life who cares about how I feel is very important to me. And as I get older, that kind of caring matters more and more. I was unconscious, though, about how deep it went.

I read Dr. Stoney's full Psychology Today article online and he nailed it for me:

If the couple does not understand this unconscious, interactive dynamic, they will think they have a "communication problem" and will likely continue to provoke anxiety and shame in each other as they try to talk. They will begin to think that they have a bad, insensitive, or selfish partner, and eventually give up on the relationship without understanding the primitive emotional mechanism that did the real damage.

First, they must train themselves to remember that they care about each other even when they disagree.

Whew! A breath of fresh air.

Stosny had a lot more to say in the article. Particularly helpful for me were his comments about how either partner can become critical, defensive, or contemptuous of the other when the primitive hardwiring is short-circuited.

I can see now how it happens in my intimate relationships: If the threat of disconnection is always lurking, it's no wonder that

PART ONE

I fight to keep the pain away. Fights are a deeper phenomenon than I'd thought. It's almost as if they are secret codes in a language buried in our human past. It's a language of pain, loss, and loneliness. And it's a language that we'd rather not experience.

So, are we fighting about *that ol' thing again?* You bet we are.

PART ONE

What Love Looks Like to Us Now

I was late to learn about the 50th anniversary celebration the Northwestern University Black Alumni Association would be convening to commemorate the 1968 takeover of the Bursar's Office by 100 black students. Our takeover was in protest to the university's tone-deaf response to the racially motivated incidents we black students experienced after arriving on campus in historic, double-digit numbers in the fall of 1966. Those of us who were part of the takeover were in our late 60s and early 70s when the commemoration happened in May 2018.

What moved me most in the Facebook message from the alum who contacted us about the 2018 event was his thoughtfulness in saying "the alumni who are healthy enough to attend." Fifty years is "a long time between drinks" (to borrow an old expression), and the past half-century had seen the exuberant energy of our youth chastened by the slower-paced tempo that comes with age.

We were a group of noble youth back then and our innocence guided us to pursue the causes we believed in. I can say now that we loved the nobility of our mission and the enthusiasm of those with whom we shared the moment. Indeed, we continue to love that part of ourselves today, even as our mature years have made us more fragile.

After seeing the message on Facebook, I saw an article online about the 50th anniversary celebration of the "Summer of Love" that was being hosted by the City of San Francisco. In the article, guitarist and native San Franciscan, Bob Weir, one of the founders of the Grateful Dead, said of the 1967 counterculture moment: "There was a spirit in the air. We figured that if enough

PART ONE

of us got together and put our hearts and minds to it, we could make anything happen."

Weir was part of the youth movement of the 1960s that saw flower children and anti- Vietnam War activists converge in the Haight-Asbury section of his city. They were ushering in what they called a "renaissance of compassion, awareness and love, and the revelation of unity for all mankind." When the 50th anniversary was celebrated in 2017, Weir was 70.

Two years after the Summer of Love in San Francisco and one year after black students took over the Bursars Office at Northwestern, Shawn Corey Carter was born in Brooklyn, New York. We know him today as Jay-Z, and the billionaire rapper is now 52. He's not young anymore, either.

In 2017, Jay-Z wrote a song that became the title track on his *4:44* album and a witness to the inevitability that the changes in our lives will affect what love looks like to us. His words, written as an apology to his wife, Beyoncé, capture the thoughts of a maturing adult who knows he is different from the younger man he used to be:

I apologize
Our love was one for the ages and I contained us
And all this ratchet shit and we more expansive
Not meant to cry and die alone in these mansions
Or sleep with our back turned
We supposed to vacay 'til our backs burn
We're supposed to laugh 'til our heart stops
And then meet in a space where the dark stops
And let love light the way

I heard about the Jay-Z album as I was thinking about what love looks like now for many of us baby-boomers. The thought came to me as I was speaking on the phone with an old boyfriend (we've remained close friends for 35 years) and listening to him go on and on about something he'd seen on TV. Eventually, he realized that he'd been going on and on and thanked me for tolerating his long-winded rambling. It came to me to let him know that I hadn't been "tolerating" him at all. "I love you," I said, "and that's what love looks like for us now."

It struck me then that I must have mellowed with age and softened on the inside. It also struck me that I may be softer now because, over time, I've lost many people who I wish were here with me today. Loss is something we all know about after 50.

In *4:44,* Jay-Z writes to Beyoncé:
I seen the innocence leave your eyes I still mourn this death

I'm sure that, like me, Jay-Z mourns much at this stage of life. He must mourn the gifted talents who were so important to his art: Biggie Smalls, Heavy D, Tupac Shakur. Weir must mourn the icons who performed at that landmark concert in Monterey, California during the Summer of Love: Jerry Garcia, Jimi Hendrix, Janis Joplin. And for us black students who took over the Bursar's Office a month after Dr. King's assassination, the names we mourn are humbler ones: Milton, Elaine, Bill, Lonnie, Clinton, Gregory, Sue, Roland, Steve.

Loss marks us; softens us. It moves us to have a different relationship with death, and it moves us to have a different relationship with love, too. We lose parents, spouses, friends, partners, mentors, and – in some cases, children -- by the time we're 50. And each time we mourn a loss, we learn more about what love looks like.

To be sure, Jay-Z's relationship with death is different on *4:44* than it was on his 1998 song, *If I Should Die,* where he wrote:

Time could never mend what these cold streets
Mentally done to me too often I close my eyes

PART ONE

And see my own coffin feelin' haunted ready to leave
This world that I'm lost in my only chance
To see the seed I lost through abortion
When I'm gone y'all niggas better not mourn

When he wrote those words, Biggie and Tupac were already gone, and he had not yet met Beyoncé. By 2017 when he wrote *4:44,* though, Jay-Z was a husband and father, and probably no longer saw his coffin when he closed his eyes. In the album, he talks, instead, about dying of shame should his children think less of him for having done the things he did when he was a younger man. He wants to be remembered by them in a different way than he wanted to be remembered by his "niggas." In *4:44,* death looks different from the way it looked a decade earlier; love looks different to him, too.

And if my children knew, I don't even know what I would do If they ain't look at me the same
I would prob'ly die with all the shame" You did what with who?"
What good is a ménage à trois when you have a soulmate?

In *4:44,* he also wrote I suck at love, I think I need a do-over. If I were to meet Jay-Z, I'd tell him (as his elder) that every day is a do-over. Each day, life offers us moments that connect us to the nobility of our love. When we're younger, we may think that moments of nobility and love are commonplace. When we're older, we know they're rare.

So, Jay-Z, I offer kudos to you for sharing your story. What love looks like *does* change as we get older. I'm looking now into the mirror of my own life as I listen to the ways that what-love-looks-like has changed in yours.

PART ONE

I've written before about Nelson Mandela marrying for the third time when he was 80 years old. (Imagine how life as a political prisoner for 27 years affected what love looked like for him!) I think what he told a TV reporter after his third marriage is a big "tell," and I'll quote it here:

"I'm in love with a lovely lady. I don't regret the reverses and setbacks because late in my life I'm blooming like a flower because of the love and support she's given me."

See, Jay-Z? Even at 80, we have a chance for a do-over.

And to borrow from one of the wedding vows, we have that chance 'til death do us part.

PART ONE

Partnered at 60

I ran into two friends the other day who gave me a fresh look at what it's like for someone to be with a partner for more than 25 years. One friend was a baby-boomer woman who has been married for 30 years; the other was a baby-boomer man who has lived with his girlfriend for 27 years. I was very interested in what they had to say because I know so few couples who have been together for that long. Married couples are rare in my circle; "marrieds" who have been together for decades, even more rare.

Marriage was not a great institution for our generation; our divorce rates are higher than those of our parents. And the marriage landscape is even worse now. According to the 2010 U.S. Census, the proportion of married adults, 18 years and older, was only 52 percent, the lowest since the Census Bureau started collecting marital data more than 100 years ago.

More startling is that, in the 2010 Census, the proportion of married women dropped below 50 percent. Indeed, the number of unmarried women (including those who are separated, widowed, divorced, and never married) outnumbered married women, for the first time in U.S. history.

To be sure, many people who are classified as single are cohabiting with partners (as my friend is). Observers note that the decline in marriage was accompanied by a corresponding increase in cohabitation.

Long-term partnering – whether in marriage or cohabitation – is the point here. A lot of us baby-boomers have had a hard time with it and are altogether done with the thing. Others are logging onto the dating websites that have been designed for older adults and are still trying to find a partner.

PART ONE

My two friends are in mature relationships. Each partner in the married couple is a therapist, and their adult son has just begun his career as an engineer. Each partner in the couple that cohabits is a professional in the world of theater, and they have no children.

When my friends spoke with me about their relationships, I listened as if I were a traveler to a foreign country. They are settled, almost serene. After living with a partner for more than a quarter century, their identities are intertwined with their significant other and their separate lives are not so separate any more.

One of my mentors used to use the term, "shared identity," to describe what can happen in marriage. We are changed by those with whom we partner and become new persons, he would say. We become a living record of the laughter and tears that mold our beings in the same way that weather shapes nature's contours.

It's a deep thing, partnering is. Research says that marriage is good for us. It's associated with higher income, better health, longer life expectancy and positive effects on our well-being. It's still unclear to me, though, how (or whether) researchers make a distinction between a "good" marriage and a "bad" one. (I didn't ask my friends whether they were "happy" in their relationships.)

In his book, *About Love,* the late University of Texas philosophy professor, Robert Solomon, introduced the idea of "oatmeal" love to capture the comfort, reassurance, reliability, and emotional security of a long-term partnership. I'm learning from folks who have been in such partnerships that "oatmeal" love can be as much a life-affirming pleasure as the thrill that a lap dance might be for someone else.

There is also an inner place, though, that we keep for ourselves whether we have a partner or not. It's the private space

PART ONE

where we acknowledge to ourselves our need for love and intimacy and commit to the fulfillment of that need in our own way.

We enter our inner space to serve that need. Some will bring with them a bowl of piping- hot oatmeal, and some will bring deliciously scented massage oil.

What will you be stocking up on?

PART ONE

Getting to Know You: Then and Now

Shortly after I turned 60, I signed up for an online dating service and met someone who -- any casual observer would say -- was a good match for me. We had much in common in many areas: family background, education, age, professional experience, and even astrological sign.

Before getting together in person, we'd spoken for hours on the phone late at night and discovered that we both loved politics (he once ran for city-wide office) and poetry. We knew the same people socially, and I even contacted a mutual friend who had been one of his classmates in business school. Our mutual friend said that my online Romeo was a "nice guy."

It took real face time with him, though, to learn that he was crazy. Not the kind of crazy that needs medicine, but the kind of crazy that could benefit from long-term professional help. The information that online dating services ask us to share about ourselves when we sign up is equivalent to what's written about us in our high school yearbook. It may be factual, but it's not relevant to being in a relationship. Dating, yes. Relationship, no.

People who want to be in a relationship want to know the "real deal" about one another. And personal disclosure is how we do it. The disclosures we want when we were dating in our 20s and 30s are different from the disclosures we want as mature singles. In her 20s and 30s, a woman wants to know that the man she is dating will marry her, be a faithful family man and have enough money to care for her and their children. In his 20s and 30s, a man wants to know that the woman he is dating will be sexually exciting, faithful to him and not too demanding.

PART ONE

Neither the young woman nor the young man feels obligated to disclose who they really are. (Some young people haven't figured that out yet.) When we're young, we think that the whole relationship thing can be managed in an *ad hoc* way. In the fullness of time, we believe, the "real deal" about us will come out, and we'll handle the situation then.

When we're in our 50s and 60s, though, the fullness of time is at hand, and we want to know the "real deal" sooner rather than later. In her 50s and 60s, a woman still wants to know that a man has enough money to care for her, and a man still wants to know that the woman he is dating will be sexually exciting. What's different for both the older woman and the older man are the health issues that have presented themselves (as they do for all older adults), and the way such issues will affect their relationship.

Some of us are courageous about it. Some want to disclose that we are cancer survivors, amputees, or insulin dependent diabetics; that we wear pace makers or prosthetics; that we are in recovery from an addiction, or that we are being treated for anxiety or depression. We want to disclose such things to our prospective lover because we want to be in a relationship where we can be loved for who we really are.

I'm thinking now of stories my mature friends have told me about moments when a prospective lover has disclosed a health concern. There is my girlfriend's story about the guy she was dating whose severe sleep apnea required him to sleep with a CPAP mask to help him breathe at night. He prepared her for it before they were intimate by showing her how the machine works. Then, one of my guy friends told me about the time he was totally smitten by a woman who sat next to him on a three-hour flight. He asked her out soon after, and on their first date, she told him that she was an insulin-dependent diabetic. Similarly, a girlfriend of mine met a guy who told her about his diabetes early in their relationship. He wanted her to know that maintaining an erection might be difficult for him.

Another guy told me about falling for a woman who was a breast cancer survivor. One day, she showed him her perfect prosthesis and guided his hand over her whole body to help him get comfortable touching her. And there is the story my girlfriend told me about a man she dated who had survived congestive heart failure and wore a vial with nitroglycerin around his neck.

Important for him was letting her know the protocols for the life-saving nitro vials. The thought of being intimate with him scared her, she told me.

None of us wants to scare people away. We all want intimacy. And in our 50s and 60s we may have to call upon an old-school virtue – courage -- to build intimacy into our lives.

Sometimes it will be the courage to disclose that which we may want to conceal. Sometimes it may be the courage to tell another what our real needs are.

I'm thinking now about the courage of the stroke survivor who had no sweetheart but wanted to feel a woman's nurturing touch. He couldn't afford a massage, so he went, instead, to a nail salon and got a manicure just to feel a woman's attentive touch for a half hour.

I'm thinking, too, of my lesbian friend who also had no sweetheart, and paid for a lap dance at a "gentlemen's club."

"Touch me," The Who famously sang. See me.

Feel me. Touch me.

Get to know me.

PART ONE

Will You Still Need Me, Will You Still Feed Me, When I'm 64?

A few days ago, I called a guy I grew up with to wish him a Happy 65th Birthday. He's a good friend and we can talk about anything. He's divorced and thinking that he would like to have a serious relationship with someone – maybe even marry again. When I asked him about his plans for the future, I took the occasion to ask him what he's looking for in a relationship. "No drama. That's what I'm looking for now," he said. "It would be fine for me to be with someone who is as straight as an arrow. That's how my ex-wife was, and now I can see that I may have acted too soon when I told her I wanted a divorce. I have better relationship skills now than I had then."

I asked another divorced guy I've known a long time the same question. "I'd like my relationship to be predictable," he said. "People are not looking for someone with problems. I'd like someone who knows that life has many aspects, someone who knows that life will bring good days *and* bad days."

I had never asked this question before, and I was surprised by the answers I got. I thought the guys would have said that they wanted a good companion, someone to travel with and share life with, or someone to have sex with. Instead, they had set their relationship barometer on a standard I had not thought about before -- one that I'd like to call "Comfort and Ease."

The first guy told me how Comfort and Ease had prompted his first marriage proposal:

I'll tell you how I happened to propose to my wife. First, she was very beautiful, I was in love with her, and we had been dating for a while. Then,

PART ONE

one night, she invited me to her place for dinner. She cooked a gourmet meal for me and put a white linen tablecloth on the table with fancy cloth napkins and candles.

After dinner, we went into her bedroom and made love. That did it for me. I knew that night that I'd ask her to marry me. No one had ever done all that for me. Before my wife, I'd had girlfriends, of course. I'd go to their house, or they'd come over to mine, and we'd eat meals together. But they never made a special dinner for me like that.

Before I knew it, I was in a restaurant with this engagement ring in my hand looking at her on the other side of the table. That's when I heard a voice say, "Will you marry me?" I looked around, and the mouth those words had just come out of was mine!

The second guy had a similar story.

She put me in a warm bath when we got back to her place after my first closing in New York. She rolled a joint for me and let me relax in the tub. Then she gave me a massage that knocked me out. After about an hour, I woke up and she gave me a small plate with the shrimp salad she'd made, and offered me some of the vodka she had frozen for me. While we were eating, she went down on me and gave me the best blow job I'd ever had. After I came, she put a piece of cold watermelon on my tongue. "Wow," I said, "you think of everything!" I proposed shortly after that.

As I listened to the guys, I could hear that -- for them -- Comfort and Ease can be anything from feeding, sleeping, caring, touching, seduction or fantasy. These are sensual delights that everyone likes – no matter our age or gender.

Comfort and Ease are a platform for intimacy. And according to the psychologists who study such things, they are also basic human needs. They are so basic that we can easily overlook them.

PART ONE

The guys I talked with told me that many of their 60-something brethren are divorcing these days. Their friends told them that, during their long marriages, Comfort and Ease with their wives had been put on the back burner, and that each partner in the marriage had grown to resent the fact that these basic needs were no longer being met.

So, for those of us who are married, as well as for us who are single, let's be honest. We all want Comfort and Ease. Seriously. We may not have thought about it this way before, and it may seem crazy to ask our partner or prospective partner to join us in the exchange. But let's give Comfort and Ease a try. It's basic stuff, and when it's mutual, it can be like heaven on earth.

The Beatles got it right. They were precocious youth when they wrote these lyrics, but the words resonate as I reflect on how much we all love Comfort and Ease:

When I get older losing my hair many years from now,
Will you still be sending me a valentine, Birthday greetings, bottle of wine?
Doing the garden, digging the weeds, who could ask for more?
Will you still need me, will you still feed me When I'm sixty-four?

PART ONE

He Loves Me, He Loves Me Not

Many, many years ago when I was a little kid, I used to pluck petals one at a time from the daisies that sprang up in the grass at Dunroven Camp, the place in Pine Bush, New York that I went to every summer. It was there that I learned to ask the daisies whether the object of my affection loved me or not. (Like the flowers really knew!) It wasn't until I was older that I realized that if I picked a daisy that had an odd number of petals, the boy would love me, and if I picked a daisy that had an even number, the boy wouldn't love me.

Things got more complicated, though, when I went to high school and saw that the boys there seemed to love only the cheerleaders. In college, the boys seemed to love only the girls who would have sex with them. And after college, the young men around town seemed to love only the young women who were good cooks. I was neither a cheerleader, nor a good cook, so I went with the third option. I wanted to be loved.

Now that I'm nearly 70, I still want to be loved and we older adults are showing our desire for love in ways that have been with us all along but weren't "cool" to talk about.

The late Maya Angelou put it this way: *People will forget what you said, people will forget what you did, but people will never forget how you made them feel.* Feeling appreciated, valued, treasured, esteemed, respected and "lifted up" are feelings we all want. No matter how old we are.

I recalled Angelou's words the other day when, Eric, having heard a sharp, impatient tone in my voice on the phone early that morning, asked me later in the day what I'd said that had ticked him off so much. He was still sleepy when we'd spoken earlier, so couldn't remember the topic of our conversation. He couldn't recall what I'd said to him, but he could remember how it made him feel.

Mood between intimates is a tricky thing. While we require closeness with others for our emotional health, we also need positive "strokes" from them for our mental health. The experts who study such things tell us that our successful evolution as a species depended on us doing and feeling things that our genes liked. Our genes seem to like it when we get positive strokes from the people close to us. When people are doing "violence" to our genes, we don't like it at all.

I'm becoming more sensitive lately to how my moods affect others. So, I felt truly "busted," when Eric commented on our morning conversation. I'm learning that the tone of my voice and the look on my face are not private to me. I'm learning that my way of being in the world affects the "atmosphere" around me. It affects not only the daily life of my loved ones, but also the people I work with, share the sidewalk with, and share life with. I'm learning that how I am in the world affects how people *feel*.

One of my blog's readers posted this insightful comment a few months ago:

As a Baby Boomer I came of age at a time when being an independent single woman who did not need anyone to accompany her to a movie or a meal -- or be her partner in life --was a badge of honor – to worn with pride. While that point of view and practice made us strong and capable, and encouraged the development of an authentic self, I can see how it might be a good idea now to nudge that pendulum a little closer to center.

We've been encouraged to be self-actualized and selfish in positive ways which now makes it a challenge for us to allow others into the fabric of our lives. Others, with their quirky tastes, habits, and individualities, who don't do it like we'd do it, don't say what we would have them say, the way

PART ONE

we'd prefer they say it; others who are not constructed to our personal specifications.

But we really do need people in our lives. So, now the time has come for us Fiercely Independents to develop a new skill – making room for others. Here's where that agape love comes in handy – that allowance to be that which we want others to grant us.

I'm working on it.

The *agape* love the writer is talking about in her comment is different from the love I wanted in high school or college, or as a young single in New York City. It's different from the love I feel for my family and friends. And it's different from the love I have known when I've been in spiritual communities.

The comment tells me that I'm not the only baby-boomer who is thinking differently these days about our connection to others. I'm thinking more about it lately because my MS symptoms have affected my mobility and opened a whole new way of seeing how much I need other people.

The terms "disabled," "differently-abled," and "temporarily-abled" have richer meaning for me now. They have helped me see that we are all part of a matrix of caring and kindness. We are all "temporarily-abled," and will one day find ourselves being helped by someone else.

I can see that my sharp, impatient tone with Eric did violence to the soft part of him that he mostly keeps to himself. It also shaved off some small percent of his well-being that day. I don't want to be the kind of person who does that kind of violence to my loved ones. Neither do I want to damage my connection -- however brief – with the person who holds the door open for me at the corner store. Usually strangers, these persons are part of the matrix of caring and kindness I'm learning about now.

"Take your time," they say. "Thank you, I will," I say.

PART ONE

It's momentary, to be sure. But in my life and theirs, it's a split second that could make or mess up a whole day.

I can hear Dr. Angelou's voice in my ear right now: *"Okay, smarty, so how did you make them feel?"*

PART ONE

In What Ways are You Crazy?

This is the question that philosopher/author Alain de Botton says we should have asked our significant other in the early days of our relationship. But no! We were too polite. We didn't ask them, and they didn't ask us. De Botton is one of my favorite writers, and the article he published some time ago in the *New York Times,* "Why You Will Marry the Wrong Person," talked about a topic I've thought about a lot. His organization, School for Life, posted an animated video on its YouTube channel after the article was published that challenges how we were taught to think about love. The video is called *How Romanticism Ruined Love.*

On this far side of 50, we baby-boomers may finally be ready to hear the truth about the Romantic idea of finding a person *"who can meet all our needs and satisfy our every yearning."* In other words, we may be ready to abandon the notions about love and marriage that have prevailed in Western culture for the last 200 years.

Newsflash: The Romantic idea has not been working out so well for us.

The pre-Romantic way didn't work out either, de Botton says. When we married for reasonable non-Romantic reasons, we still faced loneliness, indifference, abuse, exploitation, sexlessness and more. Some two centuries ago, we swapped the pre-Romantic way for the "happily ever after" way and hoped for the best.

I knew that the way I'd been socialized to look at relationships wasn't going to work for me at this stage of life. I'm thinking now of what Graça Machel, Nelson Mandela's widow, had to say about mature marriage. She said that spouses who marry when they are young can be "too demanding." The words, *too demanding,* comport with de Botton's critique that in Romanticism we look for a person who can satisfy our every yearning.

Rationally, we now know that this is not realistic. No one is perfect for us, and we're not perfect, either. We're all flawed. We're all crazy in some way.

So, where do we go from here?

Exploding the myths about Romanticism is a good place to start, de Botton proposes, and the video animation depicts some popular *love-romance myths* that are ready for demolition.

It's a myth that …

We should have an immediate, physical, and emotional attraction to each other. We should have highly satisfying sex with each other forever.

We should never be attracted to anyone else.

We should understand our mate intuitively and not have to express our feelings. We should have no secrets from each other.

We should spend constant time with each other.

We should raise a family and not lose any of our sexual and emotional intensity. We should have no need for education about sex and love.

We should have a lover-spouse who is our soul mate, co-parent, co-chauffer, best friend, accountant, household manager, and spiritual guide.

Whew! Romanticism has produced a lot of suffering for a lot of myth-loving people, hasn't it? And even though de Botton calls his post-Romantic approach a "philosophy of pessimism," and the video calls it "psychologically mature," I'm for a version of loving and being loved that makes room for us to grow in compassion for our own craziness and in kindness for our partner's.

The post-Romantic way is likely to feel foreign at first, but maybe we can give it a try. The video encourages us to consider, for example, such post-Romantic attitudes as these:
1. Accepting that love and sex don't always show up together.
2. Discussing money early on, up front, in a serious way is not a betrayal of love.
3. Realizing that we are a flawed human being, and that our partner is flawed, too.
4. Making committed efforts to understand each other; intuition is not enough.
5. Knowing that each person in the couple holds a personal standard for their own dignity.

That would be a helluva start, wouldn't it?

De Botton concludes his article with a glimpse into post-Romantic coupledom that I would love to enshrine in our new thinking:

The person who is best suited to us is not the person who shares our every taste (he or she doesn't exist), but the person who can negotiate differences in taste intelligently — the person who is good at disagreement. Rather than some notional idea of perfect complementarity, it is the capacity to tolerate differences with generosity that is the true marker of the "not overly wrong" person.

"Compatibility is an achievement of love," says de Botton, "it must not be its precondition." With that, he leaves us to think about our own craziness.

PART ONE

Gratefulness and Intimacy

The 15th century Sufi poet, Jami, wrote about a common lovers' dilemma this way:
How many lovers boldly contemplate separation, fondly imagining that they have had enough of the beloved? And yet as soon as they actually experience separation, they burn up with longing.

I can relate to what Jami is talking about because Eric and I almost called it quits the other day. A term young people use today to describe their relationship status on social media is *"It's complicated."* And it *was complicated* for Eric and me.

We had been together for many years and had begun to see more wrong about one another than we saw right. Our old stuff kept coming up and each of us was convinced that the other would never change. We had given up.

Then, from nowhere it seems, I found myself telling Eric how grateful I was for the ways the relationship with him had changed me. I hadn't necessarily seen it for myself, but some friends I trusted had previously told me about it. The best way to put it is that they thought I had become a *"kinder, gentler"* person after being with him.

I believe that everything happens for a reason and that our intimate relationships are incubators for growth and change. Our intimates often see and know things about us that we don't know about ourselves. Some call these "blind spots," and our intimates can even become "intimate" with our blind spots.

There are parts of who I am that I can't see and I'm grateful to have someone in my life who can engage those parts. I'm grateful, too, for the "more of me" that an intimate

PART ONE

relationship makes possible, and it was in this spirit that I was speaking with Eric.

I thought about our gratitude conversation for days, and eventually downloaded a book on the subject and immersed myself in a whole new world. The book is called *Attitudes of Gratitude: How to Give and Receive Joy Everyday of Your Life*. It was written by M.J. Ryan who has written several books on the subject, and says that, from what she has seen, gratitude can be generated in two ways:

> *one, by a spontaneous upswelling of the heart toward the wonder of life and all its particulars; and two, by a conscious decision to practice looking at what's right in our lives rather than focusing on what's missing.*

It's the latter kind of gratitude that came to me when I spoke with Eric.

Ryan tells us about the ways she has used the conscious-decision kind of gratitude in her marriage. In the chapter called "Fall in Love Again and Again," she writes about applying at home the new practices she learned from a relationship therapist. The therapist claimed to get better results from having couples and families send a loving, grateful thought to the other person every time they felt themselves getting annoyed or angry.

Ryan says that she tried it with her husband and had amazing results. Whether her attitude changed things, or whether appreciating her husband more made him easier to get along with is not the point, she says. But since she started using the therapist's approach, they fight less and get caught up less in their hurt feelings.

Another chapter I liked a lot was the one called "Focus on What's Right." In it, Ryan challenges her reader with the question: *"What if we spent as much energy in relationships noticing and appreciating the other person's gifts and talents and the strengths and beauty of the relationship itself as we do exposing and dealing with its flaws?"*

Here, Ryan speaks about how the practices we learned as young students in school have trained us to notice what's wrong, and to overlook – or take for granted -- what's right. By the time we're adults, then, we're good at seeing what's wrong in any given relationship, work situation, or experience.

I was struck most of all by how Ryan wove together the act of expressing gratitude and good health. Good health is meaning more and more to us baby-boomers as we do our best to remain vital, energetic, and attractive.

Expressing gratitude is like a tonic for the soul, I learned from her book. It uplifts us, bathes us in hormones that strengthen our immune system, and helps us create a loving, healing space for our intimates.

And for us older adults who are watching our pennies, it's also a great bargain: expressing gratitude for what's right in our lives costs nothing and repays us in tons of ways.

PART TWO

SEX AFTER 50

PART TWO

Booty Call? But Sir, I'm 70, Black, and Disabled!

"Let's go back to your place," he said with a smile. He had edged his way next to me as I made my way down Broadway with my walker that summer afternoon.

"No thanks," I said, irritated, and trying my best to speed up. "I'm Ralph. What's your name?" he asked, walking faster.

Ralph was a white man about my age who was trying to talk to me as I walked to the bus stop. Average looking, he could have been a cleaned-up version of a homeless guy who hadn't taken his medication that day. No matter what his story was, I wasn't interested. So, I abruptly stopped walking, spun around to look at him directly, and told him to leave me alone.

It never occurred to me that Ralph might have been a "normal" guy who was simply trying to "hit" on me. I'd forgotten about this incident until the other day when I went online and saw some YouTube videos that showed how much the worlds of sex, gender, race, aging, and disability are changing. When I was younger, I would have thought of Ralph as a dirty old white man who thought of black women as sex-crazed exotics.

"What kind of woman do you think I am," I can hear myself spit at him in righteous indignation. Back then, Ralph would have been a pervert to me. But I'm 70 years old now (probably the same age as Ralph), use a walker to get around, and am far less offended about being hit on. (No kiddin'!)

There was a time when sex between older adults, mixed-race couples, and people with disabilities was seen as out-of-the-ordinary. Today, such pairings have been normalized for the most part, and many of us baby-boomers are still playing catch-up.

PART TWO

Present company included.

A couple of the videos I saw online featured Michael Kimmel, the sociology professor at Stony Brook University in New York. He is an important thought leader in gender studies, and the author of such ground-breaking books as *Guyland and Angry White Men*. Born in 1951, he told a TV interviewer that his baby-boomer generation may be the last one to observe the sex and gender norms that have existed for most of human history.

During a lecture at Dartmouth College that I saw on You Tube, Kimmel told students that the idea of women being *entitled* to sexual pleasure is a relatively new notion. For thousands of years, he said, sexual pleasure was understood as being for men, with women seen as *facilitators* of a man's pleasure. He cited the famous 1954 Kinsey Report in which only 41 percent of female respondents older than 25 reported having masturbated or pleasured themselves at some point in their lives. He contrasted that finding with the 1996 study by the National Opinion Research Center at the University of Chicago showing that 90 percent of female respondents said that they had done so. It's a big change in a short time, Kimmel pointed out.

I felt like a tourist in a new country when a friend told me that feeling pleasure had been at the top of her agenda when she was hit on by a man in his mid-70s who turned out to be a great sex partner. My friend celebrated her 70th birthday last year, and, though she looks great, doesn't think of herself as "eye candy." She was quite surprised, then, when the married physician who attended the medical conference, she was staffing invited her out for dinner. After dinner, they went back to his hotel room and spent a happy night there together.

When she called me to talk about her new lover, she thought out loud about how differently she'd behaved as a younger woman when she discovered a great sex partner. Decades earlier, she said, she would have thought of her lover as a marriage prospect, or as a boyfriend, at least, and fantasized about the two of them becoming a "couple."

At 70, though, she noted that she's not thinking about any of those things now. When she was younger, she said, she might have been uncomfortable with him being married. Today, she's more relaxed about the situation. She was married for 11 years and has no interest in doing so again. And as for the morality of it all, her motto has become: *If God wants to strike me down for having great sex with a married man, I'm good with that. I've already had a full life!*

She was somewhat curious, though, about why her 75-year-old lover wanted to have sex with her in the first place. The truth is that she may never know what she did, or said, or made him feel that turned him on; she's just happy to know that, for some reason, she'd turned him on. (Sexual attraction is a mystery for us older adults, too!)

The trickiest part for her, she confessed, was having the emotional stirrings that inevitably come up when a person has great sex with a new partner, and not having a "story" to go with those feelings. She doesn't have the story of being the "other" woman, for example, and the feelings of sadness that come with that story. Nor does she have the young lovers' story of a bright future together, and the feelings of happiness that come with that one.

What she does have, though, is the memory of immense sexual pleasure and the desire to feel that pleasure again. It's new territory for us older adults and tells us that we'll have to craft a new kind of story to go with the feelings that come up for us now.

At Dartmouth, Kimmel also talked about the impact of increased longevity on today's college-aged youth who can expect to live more than 100 years. For them, getting married in their 20s

-- as earlier generations did -- doesn't look like a good idea. At their age, having the same sex partner for 80 years is unimaginable!

The impact of increased longevity on the sexual lives of us baby-boomers is similarly vexing. The generations that preceded ours didn't live long enough to leave tips on what to do about sexuality in older adulthood. To be sure, we're beginners in the new territory my friend talked about and will be improvising our way through this newness for a while.

Baby-boomers – and especially early baby-boomers -- grew up during a time of strict conservatism about things sexual and sensual. So, we don't always have positive feelings about pleasure. Indeed, many of us had parents who thought their job was to make sure we didn't overdo the "pleasure thing." We're learning, though, from the field of geriatrics that there are important, life-enriching connections between pleasure, well-being, and long life.

Today, enlightened professionals at nursing homes and assisted living facilities are no longer discouraging sexual intimacy between residents – including LGBTQ residents. They now know that having a love interest and enjoying moments of sexual pleasure can enhance day-to-day living at a long-term care facility. Training for professionals who work at such places must now include content on how to set and enforce policies that make sexual intimacy between residents allowable, consensual, and safe.

Ironically, it's still family members -- this time our adult children -- who're trying to make sure we older adults don't overdo the "pleasure thing."

I get it. But would somebody please tell our adult kids that an old-school "booty call" at this age might actually be good for our health!

PART TWO

Jet Lag, Cut Flowers, and the "Little Blue Pill"

One of my first interviews about intimacy was with a urologist friend of mine who shared with me some of the experiences his patients encountered with the erectile dysfunction therapies he prescribed for them.

He told me, for example, about the man who went into the bathroom adjoining the bedroom he shares with his wife to apply the penile ring that would help him to raise an erection. When he was fully erect and approached the bed where his wife was already lying down, she looked down at his erection with astonishment, and asked him where he had gotten the hard on. She was not impressed. My doctor-friend learned from that story to always include the patient's partner in any discussions about ED therapy.

Among his therapies, of course, was Viagra, the diamond-shaped "little blue pill" that has the name of its manufacturer, Pfizer, inscribed on it. The superstar of erection medications, its use has been associated with such celebrities as Senator Robert Dole, radio host Rush Limbaugh, and Hollywood actor Michael Douglas. My friend's patients were iffy about using the drug, though. Some were delighted that they could date with the gusto of their younger days, and thrilled that they could "wow" women with the endurance that accompanies an erection that lasts for hours. Others, not so much.

The urologist also told me about the couple who came in to see him the day after the man had taken Viagra for the first time: They went to bed waiting for something to happen and fell asleep while they were waiting. They didn't engage in foreplay but expected an instant erection. My doctor-friend explained to them that while Viagra might set the physiological stage for arousal, erections are still pretty much old-school and are achieved the old-school way. So, after he gently reminded them about the importance of foreplay and stimulation, they had intercourse the next night for the first time in three years.

The urologist now tells his patients the hard (pardon the pun) facts about Viagra: *it is not an aphrodisiac, it takes about 1-2 hours to work, it doesn't work for everyone, and the erections it raises may not be as firm as you want them to be.* The same is true of the other pills marketed today for ED.

Viagra is known generically as Sildenafil, and in 2017 became available in its generic form from drug companies other than Pfizer. It began life, however, in 1993, as a medication formulated by Pfizer to treat angina (chest pains) by increasing blood flow to the heart. Pfizer's research revealed that, although the drug wasn't effective at increasing blood flow to the heart, it was great at increasing blood flow to the penis. Patients had alerted researchers to this "unintended effect" when they were reluctant to return their leftover pills.

So, the people at Pfizer sought FDA approval for the use of Sildenafil to treat ED, and an immensely successful product was born. Executives at Pfizer attached to it a name that had been circulating in the marketing department for a while. They combined the words "vigor" and

"Niagara" (as in the Falls) to name the new drug that would enjoy the fastest sales takeoff the pharmaceutical industry had ever seen. U.S. pharmacies dispensed more than 215,000 prescriptions in the first four weeks of its availability in 1998, and Pfizer's stock took off like a rocket. Leaving no stone unturned, Pfizer requested -- and secured -- an unofficial blessing for Viagra from the Vatican.

Scientists wanted to know what else Sildenafil could do, and international research on Viagra boomed after its commercial debut. In 2007, for example, the prestigious journal, *Proceedings of the National Academy of Sciences of the United States of America*, published a research paper by three Argentine neuroscientists reporting their discovery that Viagra aided jet lag recovery in hamsters. And Israeli and Australian researchers discovered that one milligram of the drug dissolved in a vase of water extended the shelf life of cut flowers, making them stand up straight for up to a week beyond their natural life span.

By 2008, *The Washington Post* reported that CIA officers on the ground in Afghanistan were giving little blue pills to ageing tribal chieftains to induce them to divulge Taliban troop movements and supply routes. In one case, a 60-year-old warlord who was struggling to satisfy his four younger wives was also holding back information that could be crucial to American interests. After taking Viagra, he furnished the CIA with invaluable details. And then asked for more pills.

When TIME magazine published its cover story about Viagra when the drug was first brought to the general market, the Time.com website offered a page of reflections from guest commenters, including Bob Guccione, publisher of *Penthouse* magazine.

In his commentary, Guccione maintained that male erectile dysfunction was more a symptom of women's emasculating behaviors than men's increasing age or declining health. "Feminism," he said, "has emasculated the American male, and that emasculation has led to physical problems." Viagra, for Guccione, promised to "free the American male libido," and "undercut the feminist agenda."

Yeah, Viagra was all that.

But here's the thing: Older men aren't using erectile drugs in anywhere near the numbers experts anticipated. Of the hundreds of thousands of men who filled Viagra prescriptions when the drug was first available, only about a third obtained refills. The men who overwhelmingly support the robust sales today of Viagra and other erectile medications are men in the porn industry who pop the pills like candy, and men under the age of 50 -- both straight and gay – who use them for "erection insurance."

And while as many as half of all men over 40 experience some ED, only about 15 percent ever try erection drugs, let alone become regular users.

Why?

Because couples who remain sexually active as older adults eventually evolve away from vaginal intercourse. As a result, they no longer *need* erections. They know they can have satisfying orgasms without them.

Such an evolution takes time, though.

Most of our images of the sex act come from Hollywood sex and pornography, both largely focused on penis-in-vagina intercourse. And from the activities we see in movies, we have crafted a worldview that limits the range of erotic possibilities we imagine and fantasize about.

I'm not trying to put ED pills out of business, but my recommended drug of choice for us older adults is the intoxicating brew of the exquisite, breathtakingly pleasurable love potions we concoct for the one who turns us on.

And that magic elixir *can't* be put into a pill.

PART TWO

Condoms, Anyone?

S ome time ago, I read an opinion piece in the *New York Times* about the rapid increase in sexually transmitted infections (STIs) among adults 65 and older. It was written by Dr. Ezekiel Emanuel, oncologist, bestselling author, and vice-provost at the University of Pennsylvania, who was signaling an alarm to sexually active older adults and the clinicians, counselors and advocates who work with them. Emanuel told readers what subject-experts are saying about why STIs are on the rise within this age group. It's an unprecedented confluence of developments that we didn't see coming.

Here's the picture:

Today, older adults are living longer, are in better health, are more likely to be single, and are remaining sexually active longer. They're living in retirement communities, assisted living facilities and nursing homes where they "mingle" with other older singles. And while the older men might be using Viagra and similar drugs to maintain erections, they are less likely than men in their 20s and 30s to use condoms. Older men and women grew up and became sexually active before the era of "safe sex," and never integrated condom use into their sex practices. They think condoms are for other people -- not for them -- and are infecting each other at alarming rates.

As a generation, we baby-boomers thought sex was a risk-free activity. It was during our adolescence that the introduction of the birth control pill mitigated the threat of unwanted pregnancy. Earlier, the debut of penicillin during World War II became the fix for the bacterial venereal diseases like syphilis and gonorrhea that had vexed humans for centuries.

PART TWO

So, with pregnancy and disease neatly addressed, there was no need for condoms. Or so we thought. But in the mid-1980s, the AIDS epidemic scared us all. Even if we didn't personally know someone who had died from the disease, everyone heard of someone famous who had. It wasn't until 1985, the peak of the epidemic, that the HIV virus was isolated in laboratories, and identified as the communicable agent that could lead to AIDS.

We learned then that the HIV virus lives in four fluids – semen, vaginal fluid, blood, and breast milk. We learned, too, that we can pass HIV infection to each other through sexual contact, broken skin, blood transfusions, previously used syringes, and breast feeding. We also learned that HIV is a virus, not a bacteria, and that the antibiotics used for other STIs will have no effect on it. And more, we learned that latex – the material used for condoms -- is an effective barrier against infection, and that unprotected sex is risky sex.

The era of "safe sex" was upon us.

About that time, I began writing grant proposals for an HIV/AIDS organization here in New York. I figured that if I were going to talk the talk about AIDS prevention, I'd better walk the walk, too. I had my first HIV test to learn my status, was taught how to use a condom properly and learned that I shared responsibility with my partner for putting the condom on securely and for keeping it secure. I wrote funding proposals for another AIDS organization in 1996, and for another in 2009. For several decades, I was close to HIV/AIDS statistics, and can tell you that condom use among all sexually active groups has decreased HIV infection rates.

Now, back to us older adults: According to the Centers for Disease Control and Prevention, chlamydia and syphilis have been increasing among people 65 and older for more than a decade. These are bacterial STIs that can be effectively treated with antibiotics. They can also be prevented by using condoms.

So, why should older adults get sick from STIs when they don't have to?

In his opinion piece, Dr. Emanuel suggests that we won't get sick if we all think proactively about the problem. In his article, he proposed the following:

1. Older adults can learn the same "safe sex" practices that young people are learning.
2. Health care providers can screen older patients for STIs when they examine them.
3. Safe sex counselors can be more involved in retirement communities and assisted living facilities, and such facilities can make condoms readily available.
4. Condom makers can send free samples to every Social Security recipient.
5. Such entities as AARP and the Social Security Administration can be part of a big public health campaign on safe sex for older adults.

But wait a second! From what I hear, there's no reason to conclude that older men are having sex only with older women, or that older women are having sex only with older men. When you have unprotected sex, you are having sex with not only your partner, but with the other partners your partner has had.

So, what to do?

We baby-boomers are pioneers in many ways. We turned the Establishment on its head as we passed through earlier stages of the life cycle. Why should this stage of older adulthood be any different?

If our health care providers are skittish about discussing our sexual health issues with us, let's support them in treating us as "whole persons." If the institutions we turn to for mental, emotional, and spiritual sustenance won't take account of our full humanity, let's engage them forthrightly about the part of our being that responds to pleasure and affection.

Let the world know that we want to be touched, we want to be stroked, we want to make love -- and *we don't want to infect each other*. We don't want to make each other sick.

Those of us who are parents had "the talk" with our children when they reached an appropriate age. It's now our turn for "the talk."

Let's talk about safe sex for older adults.

PART TWO

Sex Ed for Grownups, or Who Knew?

I listened in on a webinar some time ago called "Sex Ed for Grownups." It was sponsored by the National Multiple Sclerosis Society, and co-led by a urologist who specializes in female sexual medicine and a clinical psychologist who specializes in sexual health. That week, I also got an email from the Women's Health Network with the subject line, "Low Libido in Menopause." The two pieces exposed me to sexual information I didn't know.

The urologist began the webinar by telling us how much things have changed since he started practicing medicine years ago. A woman in her 70s came to see him early in his practice, he said, with a bladder issue, and she also had a question about sex performance. He said that when he was a 30-something physician he would have thought: *She's old enough to be my mother and shouldn't be having sex at all. My mother doesn't have sex!*

Today, he's different, doctors are different, and mature sexuality is different. Penis-in-vagina sex isn't the only kind of sex people have, he says. Indeed, he's currently seeing a couple in their 80s who enjoy sex together a lot. The man is a cancer survivor who doesn't have full erections, and his wife is a survivor of two hip replacement surgeries and has joint pain from arthritis. They manage to satisfy each other quite well, they say -- several times a week.

During the webinar, the psychologist introduced us to an array of products and toys that can spice up our sex lives whether we're survivors of chronic illnesses. The products discussed included a penile sleeve that adds both length and girth to the penis; the Intimate Rider that comfortably "seats couples who refuse to let physical challenges get in the way," an ergonomic vibrator, and remote-controlled wearable sex toys (like panties) that can add an element of surprise to foreplay.

The psychologist stressed the importance of seeing sex as an ADL – activity of daily living – and talked about the health benefits of *solo sex,* or masturbation. Some of the toys she introduced are good for not only turning our partners on, but for turning ourselves on, too.

To my surprise, both the urologist and the psychologist talked about kissing and foreplay. I hadn't heard the term "making out" in decades, but that's what the psychologist called it. The urologist called foreplay "the best lubricant in the world," and the psychologist recommended lubrication for anyone at any age who has sex -- even if you think you don't need it. (She's obviously a lubrication fan!)

When I read the piece from the Women's Health Network, I was struck by how finely tuned a woman's body is to the hormones that juice around her insides. It's conventional wisdom that a woman's loss of libido, arousal, or orgasm -- and the vaginal dryness and irritation that often accompany menopause -- are linked to her fluctuating hormone levels. Until I read the article, though, I wasn't aware of certain nuances.

For example, I had not previously known that a low-fat, high-carb diet starves our bodies of the nutrients needed to make sex hormones. The article also said that the estrogen needed for vaginal lubrication is made from cholesterol. And cholesterol is often lacking in the low-fat diets that doctors are recommending for people over 50.

Finally, both the urologist and the psychologist presented us with a challenge: When mature partners can no longer expect an orgasm or ejaculation to signal the culmination of sexual activity, how will they know when the sexual encounter is complete?

During the webinar, the co-facilitators discussed the need for partners to have a way of tweaking their sex roles and arriving at a definition of what satisfying sex will be for them and their partner. They said that such frank interaction could reduce a lot of the stress and anxiety mature partners might feel.

When we were in our 20s, 30s and 40s, the narrative of a sexual encounter was built into our bodies. There was a beginning, middle and end, and you could put the sex experience on autopilot if you wanted to. At the end of the encounter, everyone would have an orgasm (or pretend to have one) and ask, "How was it for you, darling?"

Now that we're all grown up, things aren't as automatic as they used to be, and the arc of a sexual encounter isn't as obvious as it used to be. Many of won't have the dramatic orgasms of our youth to signal the climax of a sex act. So, we'll have to find new ways to let our partners know that we're "complete."

It looks like we older adults will be educating ourselves about sex for a long while. Who knew?

PART TWO

Make My Toes Curl, You Rascal You!

A while ago, there was this Associated Press headline about baby-boomers and sex:
No Satisfaction: Boomers Unhappiest over Sex. Here's the lead paragraph from the article: *"Baby boomers are the unhappiest age group when it comes to their sex life. Yet, a majority of boomers think they've learned just about all there is to know on the subject — and more women than men are confident of their knowledge. Among people aged 45 to 65, 59 percent of women think they know all about sex, while just 48 percent of men share that confidence level."*

The article was reporting on the AP-LifeGoesStrong.com Poll from October 2010 in which baby-boomers and other adults were surveyed online about their sexual satisfaction. Baby-boomers were not as satisfied as the others, though. Nearly a quarter of them said they were dissatisfied, compared with 12 percent of the 18–29-year-olds, 20 percent of 30–44-year-olds, and 17 percent of those over 75.

What's up? Was the "sex, drugs and rock'n'roll" generation unhappy because we ain't what we used to be, or were our heightened expectations about sex shaped by a time that has come and gone?

Hard to say.

Both men and women baby-boomers grew up believing that it was a virtue to be a good lover. It was good to be sexually attractive to prospective partners and master the sexual signaling we ritualized at the love-ins, rock festivals, discos, singles bars, and courtship venues of our time. It was good to be seen as a possibility for a sexual encounter, and to be "picked-up" by an admirer.

PART TWO

Today, the sexual narcissism of our generation is coming to terms with nature, the mirror and time. We acquaint ourselves each day with the subtle and not-so-subtle changes in our bodies. We are no longer tight and flat; we are round and spongy. Our lines have deepened, and our chins have doubled. We don't turn heads the way we used to.

And yet, even as our sexual attractiveness changes or wanes, we yearn for the intimacy and erotic excitement of a partner *who wants to be with us*. We long for the tenderness of companionship, and the comfort of closeness; we want to touch and be touched. We aspire now not so much to show what great lovers we are -- but to *connect*.

That we are choosing to connect sexually is a good thing. Sex is good for us. It stimulates the immune system, creates pleasurable body sensations, produces endorphins -- the body's natural tranquilizers -- and keeps male and female genitals healthy and strong.

Expressing the mature intimacy and connection we yearn for as older adults will call for a different set of sexual virtues than those of our youth. In the next decades, baby-boomers will pioneer a new world of sex, eroticism and intimacy based on the possibilities and challenges we uncover as we age.

Indeed, it'll be another kind of sexual revolution for us. The progressive sexual behaviors and attitudes we pioneered in the 1960s were enshrined in our generational anthem, *The Age of Aquarius*.

Harmony and understanding Sympathy and trust abounding No more falsehoods or derisions Golden living dreams of visions Mystic crystal revelation and the mind's true liberation Aquarius! Aquarius!

Ironically, our next sexual revolution as older adults may find its inspiration in these same sentiments. If we embrace the values and virtues expressed in these lyrics, we may discover that what is attractive and lovable about us in the late decades of our lives has more to do with our capacity to care than our capacity to come.

We may discover that unleashing our imagination and fantasies also unleashes our pleasure. We may discover that we can be lusty and frail, passionate and weakly. Eros is generous and animates the hearts of the erect and the flaccid, the upright and the supine.

The *mystic crystal revelation* that lies ahead for us older adults is the promise that mature intimacy, eroticism, and sexuality can be more profound and more emotionally rich than anything we experienced when we were younger.

And, for that, I'm a happy baby-boomer.

Go ahead and make my toes curl, you rascal you!

PART TWO

Have Fun and Go Shopping for Some Sex Toys, People!

Newsflash: Shopping for sex toys is now a mainstream activity. Bourgeois, even. If you go to Google, you can find "best of" listings for sex toy stores across the U.S. -- the Bible Belt included! Walmart, Target, and CVS have erotic merchandise sections right next to sections that sell toothpaste and deodorant. And you can order your pleasure from Amazon Prime and have it delivered to your home the next day!

This is incredible news for Eisenhower-era baby-boomers like me who grew up during the hush-hush 1950s when discreet brown paper covered everything from sexy pin-up magazines to boring boxes of Kotex.

I'll never forget the self-consciousness I felt as an early teen when I bought my first box of sanitary napkins at the corner drug store, and carried home the distinctively wrapped box feeling that the whole neighborhood knew my personal business. That was back when national marketers dared not mention the word, *sanitary napkin,* in their messaging. They referred to the entire women's personal care category as *feminine hygiene.*

By the time we were young adults, though, we had become the *sex, drugs, and rock 'n' roll generation,* and had thrown off the strictures of our upbringing. Today, national advertisers are using language that would have made our parents blush. Expressions like "erectile dysfunction," "painful intercourse," and "vaginal dryness" would have been considered obscene when we were kids. Such words would never have been uttered in public, let alone scripted into prime-time TV ads. These are everyday words now, and national advertisers are taking advantage of the generational change.

Ours is a group that is "redefining age," according to a 2012 study by The Nielsen Company, the media ratings firm. Adults older than 50 make up half the U.S. population now, and it looks like we'll be spending a big chunk of our money on products and experiences that rejuvenate our physical and mental well-being.

New internet sites for sex products now feature images of middle-aged models. Older women, as well as men, are buying more sex toys and pleasure products than ever before.

Indeed, several companies now market exclusively to older women. In many regions of the country, Tupperware-type parties have given way to adult toy gatherings, led by women for women customers. Older women are feeling that it's too late in our lives for us to be shy about sex or have shame about it. We want to use our sexuality, not lose it.

Sex toys and pleasure products are estimated to be a $15 billion industry globally, and sex shops in the U.S. report that baby-boomers are making up a large part of their business. Researchers attribute our increasing use of adult sex toys to easier availability, and to a cultural pivot away from the X-rated, red-light-district sex toy marketplace of bygone days. In other words, the sale of sex toys isn't as clandestine as it used to be, and you can now buy sex toys in broad daylight.

The "cultural pivot" can be seen everywhere. Nothing is as private as it used to be. Privacy about buying sex toys went into the dustbin of history when the first retailer in an upscale boutique turned on a bright overhead light and said "voila."

So, it looks like our prudish past is fading, and that pleasure is beckoning. A quick tour of the "best of" offers an overview of sex toy shops in the marketplace today:

PART TWO

In New York City, where I live, three of the top places to shop for sex toys include The Pink Pussycat, Babeland, and Eve's Garden. The *Pink Pussycat's* main focus is on couples looking to invigorate their sex lives with props, potions, or costumes. The staff is friendly and knowledgeable, and the store carries a huge number of toys, starting with cheap bullet vibrators and topping out with $100-plus extreme dildos. The shop is in Greenwich Village and has been in business since 1972.

Babeland sells female-conscious erotic playthings, DVDs, and educational books in brightly lit, well-organized stores. Babeland's three shops are upscale without giving off a snobbish feel, and staffers are friendly and helpful. At Babeland, you can rifle through colorful vibrators, dildos, strap-ons and cock rings, look at bondage gear, and stock up on lubrications and condoms; all three locations offer classes on everything from anal sex to blowjobs.

Eve's Garden, located in midtown Manhattan, is one of the city's top sex boutiques for women. It caters to the discreet shopper and less to the bachelorette party crowd. Here, you'll find high-end sex toys and contraceptives, instructional books, tantric supplements, and other aides that help women embrace their spiritual and physical sexuality.

Most major cities have shops that sell sex toys. Many of the shops have a website and a mail order department, too. So, if you see something on a website you'd like to buy, you can always order it and have it sent to you.

I've selected San Francisco and Chicago as two cities I know well to discuss the sex toy shops in those locales. The world-famous sex toy shop in San Francisco is *Good Vibrations.* Founded in 1977, Good Vibrations provides high-quality products, education, and information that promotes sexual health and pleasure. Its founder invented the concept of the clean, well-lighted vibrator store, and provides a safe and welcoming environment where customers can shop for sex toys, books, movies and attend workshops.

Good Vibrations is a woman-friendly, education-based retailer that offers sex-positive products and non-judgmental, accurate and trusted sex information through its stores, web site and wholesale private label division -- in an effort to enhance its customers' sex lives and promote healthy attitudes about sex. The business's philosophy is to help make the world more sex-positive and shame-free around sexual health and sexuality.

In Chicago, *Early to Bed*, opened in 2001 and says it all for me at its website:

> *Knowing that many women were uncomfortable in "traditional" adult stores, we felt that by creating a sex-positive, women-oriented shop, more women would feel comfortable taking control of their sexual selves and finding new ways to experience pleasure with their partners and on their own.*
>
> *In our shop, you'll find customers of all genders and sexual orientations. We serve customers as young as 18 and are happy to count many senior citizens among our biggest fans. We have couples who shop together, women who come in with their girlfriends, groups of friends out on the town and plenty of folks browsing and shopping on their own. Lots of our clients have never set foot in an adult shop before, and just as many are connoisseurs of sex toys. We try to make our shop accessible to adults of all experience levels, interests, ages, and relationship status. If you are wary of shopping in an adult store, we can make you feel comfortable and relaxed.*

Enough said? So, have fun and go shopping for some sex toys, people!

PART TWO

Am I Hopelessly Square, or What?

The Broadway show, *Kinky Boots,* won the Tony Award for Best Musical of the 2012-13 season. Based on a 2005 British film of the same name, it tells the story of a young man who saves the almost-bankrupt men's shoe manufacturing company he inherits from his father by converting the business into a maker of high-heeled footwear for drag queens. With music and lyrics by Cyndi Lauper, who won a Tony award for Best Original Score (she was the first woman in history to win this Broadway distinction), and a script by Harvey Fierstein, who previously won Tonys for both writing and acting, the production features such showstoppers as "The Land of Lola" and "The Sex is in the Heel."

A few weeks after the Tony Awards, the American Association of Sex Educators, Counselors and Therapists (AASECT) held its annual convention in Miami. The theme of the 2013 event was "Embracing the Sensuality of Diversity in Identities & Cultures," and its marketing brochure invited the organization's members to "come sizzle in the Miami sun and explore a spectrum of identities and cultures on the journey to sexual well-being."

I was feeling hopelessly square. From Broadway to Miami, gender-bending, sexual shape-shifting, and alternative lifestyles were capturing the public's attention, and I was bewildered by it all.

The Friday afternoon plenary session at the AASECT confab, for example, was called "A Journey into BDSM and Race." It was led by an African American woman – a "BDSM educator" -- who offered a 90-minute presentation described on the conference website as follows:

> *The taboos and community ethical guidelines of BDSM (Bondage/Discipline, Dominance/Submission, Sadism/Masochism), otherwise known as kink, power play, and/or leather, are teased out by the presenter. Infusing her personal narrative of being a black submissive (a minority within a minority group) in the kink world, she examines religious, cultural, and racial nuances of coming to and exploring the pleasure of power play. Participants are guided to a greater understanding of the personal and often spiritual aspects of BDSM.*

I was rudely awakened when I first learned that BDSM was the theme of the bestseller, *50 Shades of Grey*. When I learned that the book wasn't about sexuality and mature adults, I felt the way my super-square friend from Wyoming must have felt in the 1970s when she learned that Cold Duck *wasn't* leftovers!

BDSM was big at the conference. At least three workshops on the subject were listed on the schedule: "Kink Safety and Sexual Communication: What SECTs Should Know," "Working With the Kinks Within Kink: Exploring Disability & BDSM," and "Understanding Consent in BDSM Practices." For the third workshop, the description on the website read:

> *With the success of 50 Shades of Grey, a flood of curious people are accessing resources for BDSM practitioners. This heightened demand has led BDSM groups and events to respond by providing education on fundamental issues.*

Not least of such BDSM groups is the student organization approved at Harvard University in 2012. It's called "The Harvard College Munch" -- *munch* being the term used in the kink community to refer to a social meeting, often in a restaurant, where kinksters and/or kink wannabes share a meal.

The Harvard College Munch has a constitution and formal recognition from the school that allows it to receive grants, post notices, and use campus meeting spaces. At Harvard, Munch has both its supporters and detractors, and has prompted a lively debate in the campus newspaper, *The Harvard Crimson.*

One detractor who identified himself as an officer of the Harvard Republicans Club was quoted in the paper as saying:

At the end of the day, Harvard is a private institution…I understand the university feels it would be wrong to deny this group funding, but a serious line has been crossed. Allowing for such a group tacitly ignores the fact that…modern society still promotes certain boundaries. Allowing for a kinky sex group will only foster similar, if not more extreme clubs within our community.

So, there you have it: Conflict!

Meanwhile, back in Miami, the AASECT sex therapists had more than BDSM on their minds. Other workshops scheduled during the four-day conference included: "How to Ignite Intimacy and Sexuality after Cancer," "What's Love Got to Do with It?" "Sexuality and the Man with Prostate Cancer," "The Cultural Background and Medical Management of Female Circumcision," "Mainstream Rap Music Use, Perceived Peer Sexual Norms, and Early Sexual Initiation."

To ponder polyamory, or poly, AASECT conference participants attended a workshop called "Alternative Lovestyles: Working with Polyamorous Clients." According to Wikipedia, "polyamory" is the practice, desire, or acceptance of having more than one intimate relationship at a time with the knowledge and consent of everyone involved. It is distinct from swinging (which emphasizes sex with others as merely recreational) and may or may not include polysexuality (attraction towards multiple genders and/or sexes). Whew!

PART TWO

There was only one workshop about the baby-boomer cohort during the conference. It was called "Sex and Aging Out Loud," and was described on the ASSECT website as follows:

This session focuses on the challenges, delights, and shudders that come with writing and speaking about "senior sex." Participants will discuss concerns that boomers, seniors, and elders raise about their changing sexuality: the questions they ask, the challenges they face, and the misconceptions that hamper their sexual enjoyment. Throughout the workshop the presenter will offer tips and strategies for older adults and ways to address this age group about their sexual issues.

And finally, there was the workshop – "New Audiences" -- to help sex therapists grow their practices by learning how to navigate between different communities -- mainstream, kink, conservative Christian, queer, health-based, and more.

I've been talking about sexual variety for a long time, but I really had no idea about how varied the world of sexuality can be. I can't even wrap my brain around the debate now happening in Munch circles about the different kinds of kink sex there are.

I tell stories about baby-boomers. Our stories tend to be about the wild times of sex, drugs, and rock 'n' roll back in the day, and how age has nurtured in us an appetite for comfort and ease. I can see that I'm still hopelessly square, though. I'd love to open a bottle of sparkling Cold Duck, slip into a soft tee shirt, and ask my sweetie to rub my feet.

I think that'll be kinky enough for me.

PART TWO

"Sex Without "Sex"

Recently, I chatted with a naturopath and a sex therapist. A naturopath is a doctor who uses "alternative" healing modalities, and a sex therapist is – well, you know what a sex therapist is. The conversation focused on mature women and our bodies. The naturopath said that many of the menopausal women she treats won't discuss the extent to which sexual penetration is painful for them, and the sex therapist said that she has patients who won't have gynecological examinations because the medical procedure hurts them.

"Don't your patients know," I asked, "that they can have pleasure without penetration?

Don't they know that someone can make love to them and *not* hurt them?" The health care professionals demurred.

"You don't understand," they said, "no one wants to talk about it." Really? Well, it's time to *break the silence*.

Mature women don't want to talk about how menopause affects their sex lives, mature men don't want to talk about their erection issues, the disabled don't want to talk about the adjustments they have to make, people who wear medical devices don't want to talk about the precautions they take, and those on prescription meds don't want to talk about how the drugs they take affect their sex lives.

But we *have* to start talking *right now* about all these things.

I'm thinking now about an 80-year-old friend whose new, long-distance boyfriend came to her house to spend the weekend. He thought she'd expect him to "perform," and when he didn't get a full erection, he shook his head in disbelief, and told her that he didn't understand what was happening. *It had never happened before.* Yadda yadda yadda.

What was uncomfortable for both of them might have been made easier – and more intimate – if they had talked first about what they each wanted. Turns out that my friend would have been very happy cuddling with him on the sofa. Who knows what he might have liked?

So, when do we tell our partner what's going on with us? It may be that early disclosure will lay the groundwork for an intimacy that opens our hearts in ways we could not have foreseen.

I'm reminded now of a friend whose new boyfriend wore a pacemaker. She liked the guy a lot but was afraid to have sex with him because he might have a heart attack in the middle of their lovemaking. She was scared, but never told him. Somehow, I can't help thinking that my friend's vulnerability might have drawn her boyfriend closer, and whether they ever made love or not, her humanity and his would have been enriched.

Slowly, but surely, our generation is overcoming the misconception that intimacy means sex, and that "proper sex" means penis-in-vagina intercourse. Increasingly, as the physical challenges of older adulthood visit us, we are discovering that the simple and easy intercourse of our youth is not so simple, and not so easy anymore. And we're discovering that the sensual stimulation we want takes more time than it used to.

For post-menopausal women, mature men, disabled persons, medical device wearers, and those who suffer the side effects of medications, I have good news. There are tons and tons of online resources about "how to blow a woman's mind." Guys and gals want to know this stuff, and some websites are dedicated to describing the mind-blowing erotic activities that have nothing to do with intercourse.

Some of the intercourse-free activities listed below are also touch-free and intended to stimulate the most important sex organ of all – the brain. Here we go:

Tell a dirty story. (There are websites where you can learn how to talk dirty.) Play phone sex. (Here, you can use some of the dirty talk you learned online.) Give your partner a sensual massage. (Again, the instructions are online.)

Get a sensual massage from your partner. (Teach your partner how to "do" you.) Wear "costumes." (Use your imagination!)

Role-play. (Use your imagination!) Masturbate together. (That's an easy one.)

It's time to discover that a whole range of other activities can be just as much fun as intercourse. All we have to do is open our minds and bodies to the rewards and pleasures of a sexuality that goes beyond what we did when we were still *beginners*.

PART TWO

Making Sex Easy for Everyone

I'm jealous. Right when the sex hormones for us baby-boomers are trending downward, knowledge about human sexuality -- and the enjoyment of one's sexuality -- is trending upward. Young people today are the beneficiaries of a half-century of sex specialists talking about the subject at conferences, in research labs, and on all kinds of media. Today's young adults will get to know more about what's sexually satisfying to them than we baby-boomers did at their age.

As youth, we were the *sex, drugs, and rock 'n' roll* generation, and thought of ourselves as a sexual vanguard of sorts. We had, after all, the Pill, Roe v. Wade, Plato's Retreat, Deep Throat, the Village People, *Oh! Calcutta!,* nude beaches, sex clubs, sex-enhancing drugs, and much more. You couldn't tell us that we weren't the coolest generation ever!

What we didn't have back in the day, though, was the current body of work about *sexualities* that gives today's young people unprecedented social permission to pursue the healthy and happy sex life that suits their individual desires and tastes. They're getting the message now that there's no *right way* to have sex, and that they never need to feel shame about their body, their sexual history, or anything else about their sexuality.

During the late 1960s and early 1970s, when we early baby-boomers were still doing our psychedelic thing, the body of work on sexuality was beginning to take shape. The professional associations and journals that track sexuality research and follow trends in sexual behaviors were also being established.

In 1967, for example, The American Association of Sexuality Educators, Counselors and Therapists (AASECT) was founded with a vision to *"affirm the fundamental value of sexuality as an inherent, essential and beneficial dimension of being human."*

That affirmation, by itself, was a transgressive challenge to the sexual norms that had been passed down to our generation.

Today, AASECT's vision of sexuality goes far beyond what we could have imagined in our time. Its vision is now aligned with the expanded ideas about sexuality that have been embraced by leading international human rights, social justice, and sexual health organizations. It includes (drumroll, please) *pleasure* – both self-pleasuring and shared-pleasuring – as one of the sexual freedoms all individuals are entitled to enjoy.

One of AASECT's leading scholars (and former president) is Debby Herbenick, Ph.D. M.P.H., a researcher whose specialty for more than 15 years has been sexual pleasure. She has written extensively on the subject and has conducted many studies about it. In addition to her role at the Association, Herbenick wears other important hats. She is Director of the Center for Sexual Health Promotion at Indiana University, professor at the university's School of Public Health and research fellow at the university's Kinsey Institute for Research in Sex, Gender, and Reproduction.

In her 2012 book, *Sex Made Easy: Your Awkward Questions Answered for Better, Smarter, Amazing Sex,*

Herbenick writes:

… no one adequately prepares women or men to enjoy sex to its fullest. There's typically zero information about sexual pleasure included in most sex education programs, which means that people often learn about all the terrible things that can happen as part of sex (all the risks) but few of the very good things that can come from having sex.

The lunacy of this tactic is that, most of the time, sex results in very good things, such as feelings of fun, pleasure, excitement, connection, intimacy, love, or even the chance to make a baby. The way we talk to each other about

PART TWO

sex is broken, and it's time we fix it. People want to know how to have fulfilling sex lives, not just how to keep bad things from happening.

When I first read these words, I was delighted to see that someone had captured what I had been thinking for a long time. I agree with Herbernick that the "broken" way we talk to each other about sex needs to be fixed. Indeed, it has led to severe social consequences: It has led, for example, to a retrograde approach to sex education in public schools in the U.S. (Only 23 states mandate sex education.) And it has led to widespread use by teenagers of online pornography as their primary source for information about sex. Teens say they get more from porn than from friends, siblings, schools, or parents.

I first learned about Dr. Herbernick when I read the article, "What Teenagers are Learning from Online Porn," in an old issue of *The New York Times Magazine*. The article highlighted a "porn literacy" program in Boston, and discussed other interventions aimed at helping adolescents view pornographic content critically.

The article introduced me not only to Herbernick, but to the work of other sexuality educators – most from generations younger than baby-boomers -- whose narratives are broader than ours.

It introduced me to Al Vernacchio, the gay, Catholic, 50-something who teaches a one- year elective course, "Sexuality and Society," to high school seniors at Friends' Central School, a Quaker prep school on Philadelphia's affluent Main Line. Vernacchio is envied by other youth sexuality educators for the wide latitude he enjoys at Friends to speak honestly and positively about sex.

The New York Times Magazine published a story in 2011 about Vernacchio's class in a piece called, "Teaching Good Sex." I read it and watched several of his TED talks online. I was struck by the ease with which he speaks about sexually sensitive topics, and clearly understood why parents at the school trust him to walk their adolescents through the thicket of sex education. In his work, Vernacchio combines his background in moral theology (he used to teach religion at an all-boys Catholic high school) with his understanding of human sexuality.

Vernacchio and Herbernick are well-respected, nationally known sexuality educators who we older adults can learn from. They're from the new generation of sex educators whose work is informed by the acknowledgement of pleasure as a key feature of sexual activity. This is where their approach to sex education differs from the old-school explanations, we baby-boomers grew up with, and it's where the understanding of human sexuality is headed today.

The 21st century is ushering in new knowledge about the human brain, embryology, anatomy, neurology, adolescent psychology, and more that challenges previous understandings about our sex lives. These new insights make it difficult for us to hang onto old norms. Both Vernacchio and Herbernick, for example, want to help adolescents and other newcomers to having sex understand that most females don't have orgasms by penetration alone. To the extent that female anatomy is better understood now, these sexuality educators want their students to know about the role of the clitoris in female orgasm. Such knowledge can help young women *and* young men learn that clitoral stimulation might require oral sex, fingers, sex toys, or other devices that many in our generation thought of as no-no's. On this topic, Herbernick says: "It's part of human life, and you teach it in smart, sensitive ways."

Importantly, these educators draw a distinction between *sexuality* -- the physical, emotional, and psychological capacity all humans are born with -- and *"having sex"* -- the range of activities that individuals can engage in to express their sexuality. Threading the needle to teach adolescents how to avoid harm while helping them to develop into healthy and happy adults is the challenge of sexuality educators today.

We baby-boomers are now in our 50s, 60s and 70s, and are still sexual beings. And if we're willing to think of ourselves as *students,* there's a lot we can learn from today's progressive sex educators.

The good news is that we still have time to enjoy the pleasures inherent in our sexuality. We may not talk about it or think about it as much as we used to, but our sexuality is a precious part of our human experience and deserves to be taken care of with thoughtfulness and respect.

PART TWO

Do I Really Have to Go into a Nursing Home to Get Some Action?

A lawsuit was filed several years ago in Long Island by the adult son of an 86-year-old, wheelchair-bound woman who lives in a nursing home where the residents voted to hire a male stripper as entertainment one afternoon in the facility's rec room.

"A disgraceful sexual perversion," said the attorney for the woman's family, as he characterized the episode at the news conference, he held outside the facility to announce the suit.

"Bernice Youngblood has lived 86 years as a traditional Baptist, hard-working, lady," he said. "And now she has been defiled."

The attorney was standing in front of a billboard-sized copy of the photo her son discovered in his mother's night table. Snapped by someone on the nursing home staff, it depicts the male stripper dancing in front of Youngblood as she puts money in his waistband.

"He had a fistful of dollars in his hand," the attorney said, "and she was putting a dollar in his pants at his demand. He's leaning over her. He's not just standing there; he's intimidating her. This might be great for 32-year-old single girls, but this is an 86-year-old traditional, African American woman who doesn't want white men sticking their private parts in her face."

"There's too much sex and craziness that's going on," Bernice Youngblood's son said at the news conference. "Now they're bringing it to the nursing home, and it don't belong here."

The lawsuit says that the plaintiff has partial dementia and was shaken up when the stripper approached her and directed her to "place her hands about and upon his body, including his genital area." It says that she "was placed in apprehension of imminent, offensive, physical harm, and was confused and bewildered as to why a muscular, almost nude, man was approaching her and placing his body and limbs over her." The multimillion-dollar suit claims that the stripper incident made the plaintiff suffer extreme emotional distress, mental anguish, shame, humiliation, a diminished sense of self-worth, and loss of dignity.

According to her son, she has Alzheimer's and advanced dementia, and her confinement to the wheelchair made it impossible for her to fend off the stripper. The nursing home's attorney has challenged the claim about Ms. Youngblood's dementia. He notes that she previously signed a power-of-attorney document at the facility asserting that she was fully competent to make decisions for herself. The facility's attorney also said that a 16-member resident committee had requested the performance, and that the nursing home had paid the $250 fee.

"These are adults who wanted to have this activity," the attorney said. "They requested it, they voted on it and the nursing home approved it."

The staff said that Ms. Youngblood seemed to enjoy herself at the event and had been chaperoned that day by her other son's live-in girlfriend who also appears in the photo. With relatives at her side on the day of the news conference, Youngblood mumbled in a barely audible voice that she'd felt "terrible" and "ashamed" about what happened but could not remember the details.

Good for you, Ms. Youngblood!

I laughed out loud when I first saw the story on the local news. It turns out that in the Wise Boudoir workshop that week, we had "fast-forwarded" our lives and composed letters from our

85-year-old selves to our present-day selves to offer encouragement and advice.

"Live life and love life's pleasures" was the advice our elder selves gave us, and we took a vow among ourselves to never be too old to feed our pleasures.

I was watching an animal show on public television a while ago and saw how much animals love pleasure. The program showed researchers sending electric impulses to the parts of the brain that control pleasure in several different species. Researchers learned from their experiments that some animals would rather feel pleasure than eat.

Pleasure is very important to humans, too, so the residents at the nursing home voted for it when they hired the male stripper. And while it may be hard for me to imagine what it might be like to have memory loss, it's not at all hard to imagine keeping a hot photograph of a naked man in my night table to remind myself of the fun and pleasure I'm determined to have for as long as I possibly can.

PART TWO

Looking for New Christmas Moves?

Christmas was only a few days away, and I still hadn't gotten a gift for Eric. Since the funds weren't there to buy new, electronic gizmos or other fancy gifts, I decided on the lower- cost option of surprising him with what I called "My New Christmas Moves."

I had tons of books about love, sex, relationships, and intimacy, so I went straight to my library for inspiration, and consulted three how-to books for ideas: *The Complete Idiot's Guide to The Art of Seduction; The Complete Idiot's Guide to Intimacy;* and *Flirting for Dummies.*

Surely, I thought, there'd be something in at least one of them to make our Christmas merry and bright. As I skimmed the advice sections, though, I realized that the tips I saw were not exactly for folks over 50. So, I knew I'd have to improvise.

The Complete Idiot's Guide to the Art of Seduction was written by an author who refers to herself as "The Love Coach." Her name is Janet O'Neal. And even though most of her book is aimed at people who are young and still trying to figure out the whole dating thing, she has one chapter toward the end of the book that is good for all ages. It's called "A Seductive Potpourri: Tips and Tricks to Make the Night Complete."

Ah, yes, now we're getting somewhere, I thought. Jingle all the way! The key phrase for me was "shivers of delight" as she catalogued the "nerve-rich areas" of the body, and listed all the wonderful things that can be done to stimulate them. Okay. Into my shopping cart went "shivers of delight" and "nerve-rich areas."

PART TWO

The Complete Idiot's Guide to Intimacy was written by Dr. Paul Coleman, a psychologist and relationship therapist. His book has a chapter called "Hot Intimacy," where he tells the reader "How intimacy can go from warm to hot in mere seconds." Chestnuts roasting on an open fire, anyone?

Coleman writes:

Hot intimacy is body-to-body closeness but with extra spice; it is warmth and caring but with a delectable, playful edge; it's one-on-one connection but with an added hormonal oomph.

Okay. Into my shopping cart went "hot intimacy" and "hormonal oomph."

Flirting for Dummies was written by an author who calls herself the "Flirt Guru." Her name is Elizabeth Clark, and she has drawings and photographs in her book that let you know she's writing for younger readers. Nonetheless, her book has a chapter called "Making the Next Move" that talks about the "dizzying heights" to which a relationship can soar if a couple is "chemically compatible." Santa, Baby, hurry down the chimney!

Clark writes:

You can enhance this connection with your pheromones, the sex hormones released from the armpits and groin area. Pheromones are odorless chemical messengers secreted by animals and humans that the nose picks up at a subconscious level, telling the other person that you're sexually attracted to them.

Okay! So, into my shopping cart went "dizzying heights" and "pheromones."

My new Christmas moves were taking shape. I could see the picture before my eyes. There I'd be stimulating nerve-rich areas, unleashing my pheromones into the air, and adding hormonal oomph for an evening guaranteed to transport us to dizzying heights, inspire hot intimacy, and arouse shivers of delight. Oh, oh, Star of Wonder!

PART TWO

My low-cost gift option was richer than I'd imagined. After all, we humans, come from "The Great Manufacturer in the Sky" already equipped with nerve-rich areas, pheromones, and the possibility for hormonal oomph. These are some of the gifts we can enjoy all year.

To complete my new Christmas moves, I set the scene: It's Christmas Eve. The tree is lit up with lights that look like diamonds. A large, pine-scented green candle burns, making the living room smell like an evergreen forest. Christmas music streams from the speakers, and mistletoe hangs over the door. There is a small tin of caviar and caviar-fixin's on the cocktail table. There are two bottles of chilled champagne, and I've already poured two glasses for us. There are two Santa hats. (That's all we'll be wearing.)

That night, I was enveloped in a cloud of pheromones, and released these chemical messengers into the air as I lifted my arms to adjust our hats, straighten the hanging mistletoe, and raise my glass to offer Eric a toast.

"Merry Christmas, baby," I said.

"And a very Merry Christmas to you, too, my sweet."

PART TWO

Romance 2.0

What is "Romance 2.0?" Well, simply put, it's the way we baby-boomers over 50 are doing things in our own special way in the areas of sex and romance. I've said it before: every time we baby-boomers pass through a stage of the life cycle; we leave our mark.

The powers-that-be, it seems, are very interested in our baby-boomer boudoir habits and are spending a lot of money to find out what we're doing between the sheets. Researchers began studying us a long time ago to get the inside track on a subject that had previously been taboo -- so much so, that many older adults didn't even talk to their spouses or doctors about their sexual issues.

The 2005–2006 National Social Life, Health, and Aging Project (NSHAP) was the first nationally-representative survey of men and women aged 57 to 85 to focus on intimate social relationships, marriage, family, social ties, and sexuality. Its central hypothesis was that people who have high-quality intimate social and sexual relationships will age better in terms of health and well-being than those who don't.

Funded by The National Institute on Aging, the federal agency that supports research on older adults, the survey became the first of its kind to delve into our sexual attitudes, behaviors, and problems. It looked specifically at sexuality because sexual problems can be a warning sign for diabetes, heart disease, infections, cancer or other health matters, and untreated sex issues can lead to depression, social withdrawal, or other mood disorders.

These linkages have implications for health care providers, insurance carriers, Medicare and the sundry service providers that take care of the needs of older adults. The implications can be significant when we consider that some people even stop taking medications, they actually need because of the sexual side effects of the meds.

Anecdotally, researchers and clinicians had already found that people from the World War II era (our parents' generation) didn't want to respond to questions about their sexual activity. Such questions were too intrusive, they felt. But, unlike our parents, baby-boomers do want to talk about sex, and our response to surveys like the NSHAP has broken new ground. (Our talking about sex makes our children and grandchildren blush, though. Too Much Information, they say.)

So, while the conventional wisdom professed that people stopped having sex after some "vague" age, the survey found that although sex and interest in it did fall off when people were in their 70s, or had some chronic health concerns, more than a quarter of those up to age 85 reported having sex in the previous year.

And that's a good thing, according to the survey. It overturned stereotypical notions that physical pleasure is just for young people and became the linchpin for understanding how baby- boomers differ from their parents when it comes to sex. Consider the sexual enhancement drugs for men, online dating sites for over-50 singles, and Hollywood movies that deal with sex for older adults to witness the extent to which we think differently from previous generations.

One urologist who commented on the study said that his patients from the World War II generation were more accepting of getting older and no longer having erections. They felt that the change in their sexual capacity was part of life and shrugged it off.

The urologist's older patients today are from the Vietnam era, however, and came of age at the time of free love and the Sexual Revolution. They expect more pleasure out of life than their fathers.

Indeed, companies that make such drugs as Viagra, Cialis and Levitra have succeeded in eliminating the term "impotence" from our sexual vocabulary. We now use the term "erectile dysfunction" or ED to talk about what our fathers called "impotence." These companies have aggressively advertised their products on billboards and TV commercials, at sports events, and in men's magazines, and made ED easier for us all to talk about.

If you look at statistics, urologists say, ED is quite common and increases with age. At age 50, about half of men notice a difference in their erections and the number ramps up from there. So, someone who is 75 has a very high chance of having ED.

It's fair to say that we've come a long way from 17th century France when "impotence" was a crime that subjected a man to divorce and public humiliation. Today, those for whom sexual vigor is still meaningful have their urologists – as one practitioner said -- to "keep them in the game as long as possible."

Here are some of the survey's findings:
- Sex with a partner in the previous year was reported by 73 percent of people aged 57 to 64; 53 percent of those ages 64 to 75, and 26 percent of people 75 to 85. Of those who were active, most said they did it two to three times a month or more.
- Women at all ages were less likely to be sexually active than men. But they also lacked partners; far more were widowed.

PART TWO

- More than half of those aged 57 to 75 said they gave or received oral sex, as did about a third of 75- to 85-year-olds. One of the survey's lead researchers observed that the proportion of each gender that reported giving and receiving oral sex "matched up perfectly, giving pretty good assurance that men and women are telling the same story."
- People whose health was excellent or very good were nearly twice as likely to be sexually active as those in poor or fair health.
- Half of people having sex reported at least one "bothersome" problem. Most common in men was erection trouble (37 percent); in women, low desire (43 percent), vaginal dryness (39 percent) and inability to have an orgasm (34 percent).
- One out of seven men used Viagra or other substances to improve sex.
- Only 22 percent of women and 38 percent of men had discussed sex with a doctor since age 50.

One of the takeaways from the survey is the "use it or lose it" factor. One researcher said, "If you keep doing it, you keep doing it. If you slack off when you're in your 40s, it's hard to pick it up when you are older."

I guess that's our takeaway message, too. "Keep doing it."

PART TWO

Love Me Tender

Last week, my girlfriend and I enjoyed an early evening picnic in Central Park. We had a lot of catching up to do and watched night fall on what had been a steamy summer day in the city. We talked about family and travel plans. About mutual friends and local happenings. About our health. By the time the stars came out, and the crickets had begun to chirp, she and I were talking about our relationships and how different it is to be in an intimate relationship when you're a mature woman.

It's rare that I get to talk with a friend about relationships. It's something I did a lot in my 20s, 30s and 40s, but it happens less in my 60s. Occasionally, my single girlfriends might tell me that they've met somebody. We'll chat about it for a few minutes, but we don't go into details the way we used to.

I was happy that my friend and I were talking this way. We agreed that what we're learning about ourselves as postmenopausal women surprise us. We are learning that Mother Nature talks to us in a different way now. She used to visit us each month with her own brand of drama to announce that another cycle of life was at hand. She's mellowed now and doesn't need drama to get our attention. She speaks to us nowadays more gently about physical and financial wellbeing.

As for the guys around us, Mother Nature used to alert them to "raise their antlers" when our pheromones promised the possibility of a sexual conquest. Now, she tells them to invite us over for dinner and to hope for some friendly after-dinner oral sex at the end of the evening. She used to make us crazy with anticipation that the guy who took our number yesterday would call today. Now, it's okay to learn that he fell asleep on his sofa and forgot.

Newsflash: We're not in control of any of these changes. When we were born, Mother Nature set the table for our futures as men and women. It was going to be her agenda, after all, and we were long- term house guests who had to follow her rules. Her agenda was simple: *multiply*. She gave us the hardware and software to do it and left us to figure out the details.

We girls were born with the total number of eggs – hardware – we'd have for life, and we each got an important "software update" from Mother Nature after the last egg dropped from our ovaries. Men our age have also gotten hardware and software updates -- even though Mother Nature has made it possible for them to make babies for the rest of their lives.

For most of human history, men and women didn't live long enough to find out what would happen at Mother Nature's party after their "software updates". Now that we're living longer, we get to find out what happens, and to write our own script for the next chapter. That's what my girlfriend and I were talking about.

Mother Nature's agenda is not just about multiplying, it seems. She wired our sexual hardware and software to our "reward" and "pleasure" centers in the brain to encourage us to hang out with each other after the "multiply agenda" has been fulfilled. She promises that we'll be healthier and happier at her party if we use our hardware and software to make ourselves and our lovers 'feel good'.

As mature women, my girlfriend and I have already learned that a guy doesn't have to be a rich, powerful stag to make us feel good and that we don't have to look like Beyoncé to make a guy feel good. Years ago, though, when Mother Nature's "multiply" agenda imprinted our brains with the ancestral drive to have the highest-status mate in the tribe, we wanted to hang out with the rich stags of the world and be as fabulous as the Beyoncés. Today, not so much.

Mother Nature has a different agenda for us postmenopausal women and we don't have the same ancestral drives we had when we were dropping an egg every month. We still want to connect with a special someone, though, and Mother Nature has wired us to feel the opposite of pleasure when we're not connecting. The word we use for that feeling is *loneliness,* and Mother Nature has made *loneliness* painful for both older men and older women. Loneliness and isolation are not part of her agenda. They're not part of the party.

But "connecting" is. It's an important part of the party and my friend and I are learning how important it is to us. We are learning that, for us, connecting is more important than status. We are learning that we still want romance in our lives. That we want to be as vibrantly erotic as ever. That we want his face to light up when we enter the room. That we want to celebrate holidays with him and blow out the candles on our birthday cake with him. That we want him to compliment us when we wear a new outfit. That we want to smell his cologne on our pillow. That we want to rub his feet and for him to rub ours.

Mothers Nature's party isn't over for us yet, and my friend and I are learning today how we want to love and be loved before it is.

PART THREE

A LOOK IN THE REARVIEW MIRROR

PART THREE

Where Were You When Slow Dancing Died?

In 1959, before the earliest baby-boomer had turned 14, singer-songwriter, Paul Anka, recorded *Lonely Boy,* a song that captured a youth's yearning for love. It was a number-one hit and became emblematic for the anguish about love that many teenagers feel. *Lonely Boy* was a slow dance record that I recall from Dick Clark's *American Bandstand*. I could see that the words had deep meaning for the teenagers who were dancing, but, at 11, I wasn't yet feeling any personal anguish about loneliness – or love.

By the time I was in high school, though, it was clear that we all felt some of it. We wanted to love someone and wanted someone to love us. Slow dance records gave us a stage on which to enact our stories about teen love. These were the blue-lights-in-the-basement slow drags where our imaginations filled the pauses between the beats with longing, arousal, and hope.

For us, love and sex were connected, and we were optimistic about both. We were innocents then, and our Saturday-night sensuality was a world apart from team sports, homework assignments and hard-to-please parents. Whether we lived in Harlem or Hartford, Long Island or the Jersey Shore, Seattle, Upper Sandusky, or Oklahoma City, these slow dances said "yes" to the closeness and intimacy we ached for.

"I mourned the death of slow dancing," Eric said. He and I were talking about our high school days late one night. He was quiet for a while, and then his memory visited a bygone time:

All week long, I'd think about the party coming up on Saturday night. It might cost 75 cents if it was at Trinity Church, or maybe 25 cents if it was at somebody's house. There were always girls you hoped would be there. So, I used to get all slicked up, and try to look as good as I could.

PART THREE

After you got there, you had to develop your slow dance strategy because you only wanted to dance with a girl who would make you feel special. You had to figure out which girl it would be and how to get her to dance with you. You had to make sure she didn't dance with anyone else on the slow record you had in mind, so you had to have a plan. You'd dance with her first on the fast records. You'd try to make her laugh and like you. You'd ask her if she wanted some punch and you'd get some for her.

You'd do all these things just so you'd already be with her when the slow record came on. And when they put on the slow music, you were transported to another world. These were magical moments, and people still remember them 50 years later.

A slow dance gave you the chance to take a girl into your arms, feel her heart beating on your chest, and feel her body surrender into yours. You'd close your eyes, and the world would be just as you wanted it to be. You'd say to yourself, she loves me; she wants me. You'd know that you were pretending all of this, of course, but for as long as you're dancing with her, you're happy -- and it's true.

That night, that girl, and that one dance make you feel special. When you come from a chaotic home like I did, and there's no one there to give you a hug, this girl is the answer to a prayer. You're in her arms, and she makes you feel that she loves you. A guy always wants to dance with a girl who'll make him feel that way.

The slow record is only two minutes long, but for those two minutes, the intimacy is sublime. You want to buy the record they played. You want to take it home to be private with it.

You won't jerk off to it, though. You'll play it and cry. You'll feel what you felt on that dance floor. You'll feel your partner. The darkness. The dim lights. You live for this feeling. It makes you feel rich.

And if the girl is pretty, better looking than the other girls at the party, you'll feel like you're the captain of the football team. If a pretty girl dances with you on a slow record, you'll ask for her phone number and find out what school she goes to. You'll offer to carry her books. If you live in

PART THREE

Harlem and she goes to school in Queens, you'll say, 'That's okay, I'll go to Queens to carry your books'. Then, she'll say, 'You came all the way to Queens to see me?' Yes! And when you carry her books, that's when you talk to her about when the two of you get married.

I'm not joking. A slow dance could lead to all that.

But, after high school, the discotheques came, and the girls didn't want to slow dance anymore. "Nobody's doing that," they said. They were sophisticated now. They were in college or had jobs. They said they didn't want to slow dance because it would mess up their outfits.

Yeah, I was there when slow dancing died.

PART THREE

The Music that Made Us Dance: Baby-Boomer Love Songs 101

I was born during the first few years of the baby-boom. The U.S. Census calls people like me Early Boomers, or EBs; we were born between 1946 and 1955. Behind us came the Late Boomers, or LBs, and they were born between 1956 and 1964. We're all baby-boomers, to be sure, but EBs and LBs are different from each other in notable ways. A startling marker for our difference can be found in the love songs that EBs and LBs listened to and danced to when we were teenagers.

The lyrics of the songs that saturated the airwaves when EBs and LBs were each 18 speak volumes. I choose 18 because it's the age by which many teenagers become serious about their romantic lives. The love songs from our teen years are important because they are the sounds we absorbed as we formulated our thoughts about intimacy and romance.

The first baby-boomers turned 18 in 1964, and cultural observers note that – musically speaking -- the early 1960s were very much like the 1950s. After 1965, though, the decade had a different character, and it's easy to see the shift in the love songs that were popular. The Grammy award for best male vocalist in 1964, for example, went to Jack Jones for *Wives and Lovers*. With lyrics that could have been written for a 1950s Hallmark card, the up-tempo waltz encouraged stay-at-home, suburban marriage as desirable for a woman, and urged her to be seductive and sexually alluring with her husband at the end of his work day.

It's a very 1950s message. Here are some of the lyrics:
For wives should always be lovers too
Run to his arms the moment he comes home to you He's almost here

PART THREE

Hey, little girl, better wear something pretty Something you'd wear to go to the city and
Dim all the lights, pour the wine, start the music Time to get ready for love

Another love ballad from 1964 that evokes the 1950s was Dean Martin's hit, *Everybody Loves Somebody Sometime*. In it, he sings about the magic of love, and hopes that every man could be as happy as he is. And there was also the album, *This is Love,* by Johnny Mathis, where he performs Broadway- and Hollywood-inspired ballads that are lushly orchestrated with violins.

The year, 1964, also gave us glimpses of things to come, though. Johnny Mathis's romantic sound and the Righteous Brothers hit, *You've Lost that Lovin' Feeling,* were examples of "crossover" music. "Crossover" meant that the same love songs were played on both black radio stations and white radio stations.

America was still racially segregated in 1964, and so were its music-listening habits. Crossover was a new phenomenon. In previous decades, Nat King Cole had been its reigning monarch, but his music was for grownups. *Nature Boy* and *Mona Lisa* didn't contemplate black teens and white teens being on the same dance floor thinking romantic thoughts. For many in America, that idea was a no-no.

By 1973, though, when the baby-boomers born in 1955 – the halfway mark for the EB cohort -- turned 18, the world of music had changed. Rock 'n' roll ruled, and R&B hits. i.e., music typically performed by black recording artists was appearing in top slots on Billboard's national pop charts.

In the broader society, the Pill, the Sexual Revolution, the Civil Rights Movement, the Vietnam War, and the Women's Movement had transformed old assumptions about gender roles and social institutions. And in the 1967 Loving v. Virginia decision, the Supreme Court had declared as unconstitutional the prohibitions in many states on interracial marriage.

PART THREE

The love songs baby-boomers were listening to by 1973 reflected those changes. For example, the 1972 hit, *Me and Mrs. Jones,* by Billy Paul, secured *Billboard's* number-one slot for three weeks at the end of 1972, won a Grammy for the singer in early 1973 and became an R & B perennial. The song depicts a married woman who is the polar opposite of the doting housewife that Jack Jones sang about less than a decade earlier. Here are some lyrics:

Me and Mrs. Jones, we got a thing going on We both know that it's wrong But it's much too strong to let it cool down now
We meet ev'ry day at the same cafe Six-thirty I know she'll be there
Holding hands, making all kinds of plans While the jukebox plays our favorite song

Mrs. Jones's indiscretions aside, 1973 was a rich moment for baby-boomer love songs. Included in that banner year were *Neither One of Us Wants to Be the First to Say Goodbye,* by Gladys Knight and the Pips; *Touch Me in the Morning,* by Diana Ross; *You Are the Sunshine of My Life,* by Stevie Wonder; and *Let's Get it On,* by Marvin Gaye. Baby-Boomer era classics, all.

The *pièce de resistance* in 1973 is Roberta Flack's number-one song, *Killing Me Softly with His Song.* The intimacy expressed in the song's lyrics takes one's breath away. At the 1974 Grammy awards, it was named Song of the Year and Flack was named best female pop vocalist.

The award reprised her 1973 debut outing at the Grammys when *The First Time Ever I Saw Your Face* was named Record of the Year *and* Song of the Year. Flack remains the only recording artist to have won those two distinctions in the same year.

If I had to choose a climax to our generation's musical love journey, it would be the 1982 recording that both completes the crossover from R&B to pop, and plants a stake in the ground for the expressive freedom our generation pioneered: *Sexual Healing*, by Marvin Gaye.

In 1982, when the youngest baby-boomers, those born in 1964, turned 18, *Sexual Healing* brought Marvin Gaye three Grammy nominations. In early 1983, he won for Best Male R & B Vocal Performance and shared a second Grammy with other musicians who were on the ground- breaking recording date with him. *Sexual Healing* became an international success, topping record charts on three continents. Here are some lyrics:

Whenever blue teardrops are fallin' And my emotional stability is leaving me There is something I can do I can get on the telephone and call you up, baby And honey, I know you'll be there to relieve me The love you give to me will free me

If you don't know the thing you're dealing Oh, I can tell you, darling, that it's sexual healing.

I talked with friends about how the music we listened to back then changed from decade to decade, and we agreed that all of it shaped our intimate lives – including the Hallmark- inspired songs of Jack Jones and Dean Martin. We baby-boomers were also the first TV generation, after all, and the family-friendly variety shows on which performers like Jack Jones and Dean Martin appeared were platforms that endorsed both the messengers *and* their messages.

The love songs we heard when we were in our teens reflected the changing rhythms in the *outside world* and echoed the changing rhythms in our inside world, too. I carry this music with me today, and whenever my memory reaches for a whiff of the girl, I was at 18, it always comes with a delicious beat and a bright smile.

PART THREE

Will There Ever Be Love Songs Again?

He's retired now, but I'll never forget former Dallas Police Chief David Brown quoting the Stevie Wonder love song, *As*, at the nationally televised memorial service for the police officers who were killed in 2016 by a sniper after the Black Lives Matter march in his city.

Before he introduced the song, Brown told the audience that when he was a teenager and started liking girls, he could never find the right way to express himself. Girls would always walk away after he'd said a few words, and he was left trying to figure out what he needed to say to hold their attention. Using his knowledge of lyrics from 1970s rhythm-and-blues love songs, though, he finally put together a strategy for getting girls to talk to him.

"For the girls I liked, I would pull out some Al Green or some Teddy Pendergrass," he told them. "But if I fell in love, I had to dig down deep and get some Stevie Wonder, to fully express the love I had. So, today, I'm going to pull out some Stevie Wonder for the families."

"Families," he said, "close your eyes and imagine me back in 1974 with an Afro, some bell-bottoms and a wide-collar shirt."

With that invitation, and with deep feeling, Police Chief David Brown quoted the popular songwriter:

Until the rainbow burns the stars out of the sky, I'll be loving you. Until the ocean covers every mountain high, I'll be loving you. Until the dolphin flies and parrots live at sea, I'll be loving you.
Until we dream of life and life becomes a dream, I'll be loving you. Until the day is night and night becomes the day, I'll be loving you.

PART THREE

"I'll be loving you always," he said.

It was in memory of his colleagues that Brown spoke to the families of the fallen, and we who listened understood his sentiments. We understood the kind of love Stevie Wonder was talking about. We had just never heard his lyrics used to memorialize slain police officers.

Public expressions of love are rare. We usually hear them during solemn occasions. As adults, we're not comfortable declaring our romantic love in public, or seeing others do it. It feels awkward. The one time, though, that public love doesn't feel so awkward is when a newly married bride and groom express their love during the first dance at their wedding reception.

It's a quintessential romantic moment, indeed, and the newlyweds typically select a love song that has special meaning for them. The songs we hear on that occasion usually come from the reservoir of love songs most of us know by heart. They are the songs we hear on the radio and dance to in discos and clubs. They are the songs we heard during our courtship and will forever link us to memories of falling in love.

In his 2015 book, *Love Songs: The Hidden History*, music historian Ted Gioia says that the future of the love song looks grim. After millennia of lyrics about love, longing, and loss, we seem to be living in a moment when love themes are fading from popular music. He writes, for example, about the "genuine sense of panic" a young guy must feel when he has a huge collection of rap and hip-hop music but can't find anything to play in the background when he brings a date back to his place after a night of hanging out on the town. Gioia tells us that romance in popular music is increasingly being pushed onto the back burner.

For us baby-boomers, by contrast, love songs were everywhere. On TV, we could watch old-time crooners like Frank Sinatra, rock 'n' roll bands like the Beatles, R & B geniuses like

PART THREE

Marvin Gaye, singer songwriters like Carol King, and megastars like Elton John and Prince.

On the radio, we could listen to top-40 love songs, easy listening love songs, country-western love songs, adult-contemporary love songs, love songs from the movies, love songs from Broadway shows, love songs from Motown, and standard ballad love songs.

We're not quite sure when it happened, but love songs stopped being in the atmosphere the way they used to be. We baby-boomers were caught by surprise because we thought love songs would always be around. After all, we'd heard them when we listened to our grandparents' music, our parents' music, and our children's music. We naturally thought we'd be hearing new love songs in our children's music. But it was not to be.

Gioia takes his readers on a tour of the music scene after the advent of MTV and You Tube and shows us how sexuality won out over romance for the young people born in the hip-hop, rap, and MTV generations. He shows us that a hit song today has to have a hit video to go with it, and that the video it comes with has to command eyeballs. Accordingly, a "hit" love song today is a video-driven creation with erotically charged imagery and unambiguous sexual oomph. Everyone understands that videos are about sex – not love.

Gioia writes that most of the songs sung over the last thousand years of human civilization have, indeed, been love songs, and that changes in these love songs mirrored changes in courtship, romance, sex, and marriage. I've always been struck by song lyrics from bygone eras where the man singing the lyric longs for the moment he can "be with" the woman he loves. When I hear those old standards, I have to remind myself that the singer couldn't "be with" his girl until *after* they were married. Establishment society looked down on pre-marital sex until just a few decades ago, and popular love songs reflected the morality of the time.

In a few of his media appearances, Gioia has told interviewers that some of the music industry people he's talked with about the book have dismissed the love song as wimpy, sentimental, and lightweight. Let the love song detractors tell that to the successful radio stations across the U.S. that have adopted "oldies" formats that cater to folks who like the old-school sound. Let them tell that to the Internet listeners who are devoted to channels that stream simple and sex-free love songs. Let them tell that to the millions who love country music precisely because it *is* sentimental and heartfelt.

And let them tell that to the folks who remember when love songs were in the air so much that a police chief could recall using Stevie Wonder's lyrics to express his teenage feelings to a girl he'd fallen for, and then use the same lyrics decades later to express his feelings to grieving families whose slain loved ones had served under his command.

Gioia says that technology -- customized playlists, personalized earbuds, and such – has done its part to separate music listening from the traditional places where courtship and romance take place. The ballrooms, house parties, nightclubs, and social gatherings where couples from an earlier time used to meet, flirt, date and dance have lost their currency.

Gioia admits that a young lover can still take his date out to hear live music or to dance, and the couple can still enjoy the seductive sounds while the lover advances his romantic agenda. But he writes, this kind of *coupled music consumption* is getting rarer and rarer.

So, will there ever be love songs again? Gioia is optimistic and looks to other changes in popular culture for a ray of hope. He thinks that the next revolution in music will be similar to

PART THREE

what's happening in food and beer, where you hear the word, "crafted," a lot. The idea of "crafted" is that the thing being described is no longer routine. It's no longer targeted to the mass market – as some music videos are. The idea of "crafted" music is that it will be more sophisticated *and* more down-to-earth at the same time.

Until the time comes for the next music revolution, though, there will still be a few young musicians, like Usher, Rihanna, Justin Timberlake, John Legend, or Nora Jones, who a guy of any age can play in the background when he brings a date back to his place.

And there will still be a few songs – here and there -- that can set the mood for romance and the time-honored wonder of falling in love.

PART THREE

Coming of Age before Roe and the Pill

The U.S. Supreme Court voted to legalize abortion in Roe v. Wade in 1973. A year earlier, in Eisenstadt v. Baird, it voted to legalize birth control irrespective of a woman's marital status. Prior to then, in many states, birth control was only legal for married women, or for women who could prove that they would be married within six months.

Seven years before Eisenstadt, at the age of 16, I became sexually active and used no contraception. At 17, I got pregnant and had an illegal abortion a few days before my high school graduation ceremony. At 18, I began taking the Pill during my first semester in college. Mine is not an atypical story for a sexually active early baby-boomer. Several girls from my New York City public high school's senior class were pregnant when we marched across the stage to receive our diplomas. After missing our periods, we had conferred many hours on the phone about -- what would prove to be -- futile strategies to end our pregnancies. Our ignorance about such things was vast.

When I realized that I was pregnant, I knew that I wanted to have an abortion. I also knew that I couldn't tell my mother anything about my pregnancy or my plan. Her South Carolina values were such that she might pressure me to give birth and let her take care of the baby. I had already been accepted to Northwestern University, though, and all I wanted to do was to end the pregnancy and start college.

I put my plan together with help from a good (Platonic) friend. He lived across the street from me and had graduated from my high school the previous year. He knew of someone who had performed abortions for other girls and gave me her name and

PART THREE

phone number. He also knew the name of a doctor who would write a prescription for post-abortion antibiotics and render medical care if I needed it. On my end, I had to secure money for the procedure, and locate a place to have the abortion performed. Fortunately, one of my girlfriends from school who was also pregnant told me that I could have it done at her house while her parents were at work.

As for the money, that would be trickier.

In 1966, the cost of an illegal abortion in New York City was $125 -- a lot of money for a high school kid. I worked weekends as an usher at an Off-Broadway theater, and that job paid $25 a week. My only stash was the $100 U.S. Savings Bond I'd received as first-prize winner in an essay contest the previous year. The redemption value of the bond at the time was only $75, and it wouldn't mature to $100 until 1979. Cashing it in would be a big deal for me.

Winning it was a big deal, too. I had won first prize -- first prize! -- in a citywide essay contest sponsored by the city's leading newspaper, *The New York Daily News,* on the occasion of the 750th anniversary of the birth of the 14th century Italian poet Dante Alighieri. I was proud to have won it. From what I can remember, 11th grade honors English classes across the city were reading the John Ciardi translation of *The Divine Comedy,* and students who competed for the prize had to write a 500-word essay on the subject, "What Dante Means to Me."

I'd had my first sexual experience during that semester and thought I had discovered the sweet mystery of life. Inspired by what I thought of as my new depth of carnal knowledge, I called my essay, "What Dante Means to Me: Lust for Life in a Vale of Tears."

In it, I explored Dante's passion for his beloved Beatrice. It was my thinking that my precocious insight into the erotic would dazzle the contest's judges and secure a victory for me. I'm not sure if that happened, but I did win first prize. The irony was that I would use the prize money for an illegal abortion.

Dante's was a courtly, non-sexual love, and Beatrice was his ideal woman. Theirs was the kind of love I longed for, but one that was not part of my story. I'd had sex with someone I didn't want to be a part of my future, so I never even told him that I was pregnant. I didn't know what to say.

Although I did have some medical complications from the abortion, I was strong and healthy by the time I left for college in September. (Ah, youth!) There, I met girls on campus who were still virgins. Many guys on campus were virgins, too. Not for long, though. We were the college generation that transitioned from having "parietal" hours -- when a young man could visit a woman's dorm room during designated times, keeping the door open -- to co-ed dorms where couples were, unofficially, co-habiting.

Sexual freedom erupted into our lives before our pastel hearts had gained full color. At 18, we might have been sexually free, but we were fragile and uncertain in so many ways.

PART THREE

Wild and Crazy Sex between the Pill and the Virus

It was a wild and crazy time to be young. Between 1964 -- when the earliest baby-boomers turned 18 and a significant number of young women began taking the Pill – and 1986 -- when the HIV virus alerted our generation to an unimaginable possibility -- sexual freedom ran amok for youth in a way that was unprecedented in human history.

We were more affluent, more mobile, more cosmopolitan, more narcissistic, and less burdened with responsibility than youth had been in previous times and places. There were also more of us -- at least 77 million -- and there was nothing to stop us from having sex with whomever we were attracted to. The Pill prevented unwanted pregnancies, antibiotics treated STIs, and we had not yet heard about the lethality of the HIV virus. Believing that we could have as much sex as we wanted without incurring fatal consequences, we were fearless. It was a time when the glamorization of "sex, drugs and rock 'n' roll" was in the air.

The world was still divided into "nice" girls and "wild" girls when I got to college in 1966, but the hyper-sexuality of our generation was well underway. By 1967 and the "Summer of Love," counterculture values about sex had become mainstream. When we black students occupied one of our college's administration buildings in 1968 with our list of demands, students outside the building who were supporting our protest provided us with condoms for use while we were holed up. We were only there for 36 hours, and never used them, but the condoms were in supply just in case.

That was College sex.

PART THREE

There was also its kissin' cousin, Movement sex, so called because Movement sex often happened on or near a college campus. Our generation had lots of movements: anti-war, black liberation, women's liberation, free speech, civil rights, abortion rights, gay rights. And there was sex to go with each of them.

For example, here's how Movement sex worked: A national spokesperson for a movement would go to a campus to give a talk and it was understood that, at the end of the talk, he (it was usually a "he") would have sex with whomever he chose. If you were a co-ed, being chosen by the national spokesperson would make you a star on campus. And other students would glow with pride when they said, "Did you know that so-and-so slept with fill-in-the- blank." That was Movement sex.

There was also Music industry sex, as articulated in the iconic phrase, "I'm with the band." So, whether you were a man or a woman, being "with the band" gave you standing. I had standing one time. I was at home in Harlem on a school break, and a couple of my girlfriends had access to visit the Temptations and the Miracles in their backstage dressing rooms at the "World Famous Apollo." We stayed in the theater until the last show was over and exited with the Motown bands through the stage door where lots of fans had gathered. It was heady stuff to descend the stage door stairs, walk past the fans, and get into the limo with Smokey, Ronnie, Bobby, and Pete. "Wow, look at me. I'm with the band!" I thought to myself.

Then, if you were actually in the band, or touring with a Broadway show, a ballet company, an orchestra, or the like, there was Road sex. And there was a thing called "road relationships," liaisons you'd have for the run of the tour. The same is true if you were in a summer stock company or on a set shooting a movie.

I once saw film director, Steven Spielberg, on a late-night show explaining to the host what he does on the first day of a shoot. He said that he gathers everyone together to read through the whole script so they can see what the project is all about. That's one reason to get everyone together, he said. The other reason is to give everyone a chance to see who else is on the project.

Spielberg said he knew that he couldn't start shooting until he had everyone's attention, and that he wouldn't have everyone's attention until people had paired up. By the third day, everyone had pretty much decided who they were going to sleep with during the shoot, and he could finally get to work.

That's how Road sex worked.

Many baby-boomers entered corporate America and enjoyed the business equivalent of Road sex. I call it Business trip sex, or Convention sex. That's where you have sex in fancy digs paid for on your expense account: The Four Seasons, MGM Grand, L'Hermitage. And on and on. So many kinds of sex, and I've just scratched the surface. We sexed it up all over the place.

Conspicuously missing from my guided tour of young baby-boomer sex are drugs, which we did a lot of. For the "drugs" part of our "sex, drugs and rock 'n' roll" story, I'm afraid I'm not the best reporter. Indeed, I was a square in that department. The closest I ever came to acid, for example, was the Timothy Leary (of LSD fame) lecture at Columbia University that I went to while I was still in high school. I was 16, had a curfew, and my mother wouldn't let me travel alone in the city at night. It was she, then, who went with me to hear Leary's talk. (She was happy to do so. God bless her!) My otherwise conservative mother regaled her friends for years, when she talked about how the "crazy white man" told us to "turn on, tune in, and drop out."

By 1984, we knew something was going on because people were dying. The disease was first called GRID, gay-related immune disorder, because only gay men were dying, it seemed. By

1986, I was writing grant proposals for a nonprofit here in New York City that delivered hot meals to homebound people living with AIDS. We had learned a lot, by then, about how the HIV virus infects people.

That year, I had my first AIDS test, and was on pins and needles until I got the report that I was HIV negative. While I sat there waiting at the clinic, I thought a lot about the unprotected College, Movement, and Road sex I'd had.

I have now been a grant writer for two other AIDS charities and had to become a student, of sorts, about sexually transmitted infections. Those of us who came of age between the Pill and the Virus lived in a world in which we could be narcissistically engaged in lovemaking, but emotionally indifferent.

"But it feels so good," I can hear our generation say.

Today, the stakes are higher. We know that lovemaking is not the sport we once thought it was. We've matured, and now know that everyone's life -- and everyone's love -- is a precious jewel.

PART THREE

Prince Charming Stories

Most women have them at this stage of life: Prince Charming stories. Sometimes the story is about the one that got away; sometimes it's about the prince who hung in there, and eventually became a grumpy old man; and sometimes it's about the one you thought was a prince, but turned out to be a frog no matter how many times you kissed him.

My physical therapist told me a doozy the last time I saw him, and said, "Do whatever you want with it in your blog. I just think it's great." The story is about a woman who'd made finding a Prince her "job."

Let me set the scene for you: Picture an upscale cocktail lounge in Manhattan where fancy people go to meet other fancy people. My physical therapist is a hot, young single at the time, and is having a drink at the bar when a gorgeous woman sits down next to him. I should tell you that my therapist is a former tennis pro of Spanish descent who looks like a movie star. So, it would make sense that a gorgeous woman would check him out, right? He buys her a drink, and they start talking.

"So, what do you do?" she asked. "I'm a physical therapist," he said.

Well, he could tell right away from her body language that his answer had turned her off. The gorgeous woman who was so eager to chat with him a few minutes earlier had suddenly lost interest altogether. Curious about the change in her mood, he summoned the courage to ask her to be honest about what she'd thought when she heard him say that he was a physical therapist. The conversation that followed was an eye-opener for him, and

PART THREE

well worth the cost of the expensive drinks he bought at the fancy bar.

First, she told him that she'd be frank with him because he seemed open to her honesty.

Then, she told him all about her game plan. She said that when he told her what he did for a living, her thinking had been that his income was not what she had in mind for her future. She was only interested in talking to rich guys, she said, and physical therapists aren't rich. She'd taken a good look at what she had to offer: She was blond with a great figure and very pretty. She knew that she could capitalize on these assets, marry a wealthy man, and be set for life.

"This package will only last ten years," she said, "so I have to stay focused. I have a 9 to 5 job that I go to every day to pay my bills, but marrying a rich man is my real job."

"Wow," said my therapist, "tell me more."

She told him that the wardrobe, makeup, skin, and hair care she pays for are investments into the business of marrying a rich guy who's looking for a "trophy" wife. The proceeds of her day-to-day job pay the "business expenses" for the enterprise. She urged him to do the math: Ten years of concentrated effort to set yourself up for a lifetime of luxury is not a bad investment, she argued, pointing out that her end game might be achieved sooner, say, in year three or year eight. She was mindful that her "trophy look" would only last ten years, though. After that, she said, you lose the edge. She was serious about her goal and about the amount of time she had to accomplish it. She had no time to waste.

"So, what does a guy have to do for a living to hold your interest?" my therapist asked. "I'm looking for a Wall Street type, a finance guy, someone like that," she said.

"And how do you figure out how much money he has?"

PART THREE

"Well, I look at where he takes me on dates and how much he spends. Does he call for a car to drive us where we're going? Does he ask me to go away with him for a private weekend? Things like that. That's how I figure it out."

"Do you ever offer to pay for anything?"

"Sure, I do. Of course. If I like a guy and want him to like me, I'll pay for dinner or drinks or something. I wouldn't want the guy I liked to think I was only interested in his money."

As my therapist talked, he and I were shaking our heads in amazement about her clarity and determination.

"So, what did you say to her about all this?" I asked. "I wished her good luck," he said still shaking his head. "What else could I say?" While my therapist was telling me this story, I was silently singing to myself the song, *Ten Good Years*. I'd heard it on an album by jazz vocalist Nancy Wilson that I'd bought while I was still in high school. Ten Good Years had been written especially for her nightclub act, and the album I'd bought was a live recording of her show at the then-famous Coconut Grove in Los Angeles.

I wanted to be glamorous and sophisticated like Nancy Wilson back then. I played her album hundreds of times and memorized the words to all the songs. *Ten Good Years* was an up tempo, snarky kind of tune that I didn't completely understand when I was younger. To be sure, it hadn't been written for teenage girls from Harlem like me. It was written to entertain the sophisticated women who saw Wilson's act at fashionable supper clubs like the Coconut Grove and knew what it meant to have "work done."

When I bought the album, I was old enough to be thinking about ways to attract my own Prince Charming. For some reason, I thought he would be impressed by my wannabe glamour and sophistication. It was, after all, the mid-60s, and my hometown of

PART THREE

New York City was aflutter with the glamour of the Supremes at the Copa, false eyelashes, and trendy discotheques. I thought that if I could look like I belonged in that glamorous world, I could certainly capture my prince's attention.

What did I know? I was a kid.

Shortly after I'd bought the album, I traveled to a Colorado dude ranch with a youth group from my church. I knew that boys would be going on the trip, so I packed as much glamorous stuff as I could. It hadn't occurred to me that my false eyelashes would be hard to apply at a dude ranch (no mirrors, bad lighting), and that having the right shade of blush wouldn't matter much there, either. Years later, I ran into a woman who'd been on that trip and remembered me *and* my makeup.

"You used to wear a lot of makeup," she'd said with scorn. "I mean ... *a lot.*"

I wanted to tell her that I was wearing it to attract my prince but felt that saying so would make me sound foolish.

It turns out, in odd way, that the trip to Colorado would teach me a lot about my Prince Charming fantasy. The itinerary for the trip rolled out over several legs, and it was on the last leg of the return trip that I had my 'aha' moment. To travel west, we had ridden chartered buses from New York to Chicago, and then ridden the now-defunct Denver Zephyr from Chicago to Denver. (I still remember the spectacular views of the Rocky Mountains from the train's observation dome.)

Our return trip would have followed the same sequence in reverse were it not for a problem with the chartered buses that were supposed to take us from Chicago back to New York. To solve the problem, about eight of us piled into a rental van, and headed east for a 12-hour, 800-mile road trip back to Harlem.

The two guys from our group who shared the task of driving the van were college juniors who had also been activity leaders at the dude ranch. I wanted to get to know them better and volunteered to help on the trip. The one thing I knew I could do back then was stay up for long hours, so my assignment became keeping the drivers awake. I sat in the van's "shotgun" seat and talked with them through the night while the other passengers slept.

It was during the long drive that night that my thoughts about Prince Charming began to shift. As we talked, I learned that one guy was from Harlem, and the other from Virginia. They were roommates at a predominantly white college in upstate New York, and one of them played on the school's nationally ranked basketball team.

For a black teenage girl who was about to go into her senior year of high school, talking to two black college juniors was a big deal. Going to a mostly white college was not common for black high school graduates back then, and one of the guys would tell an audience made up of his school's black alumni years later that students of color were less than one-half of one percent of the student body when he went there in 1964.

Things were so numerically out of whack, he told them, that when school administrators reprimanded black athletes for dating white girls, the black athletes countered by recommending that the school admit more black co-eds. A scandal arose, though, when it was discovered that only "pretty" black girls were being admitted. (That was back when college applicants had to attach a photograph of themselves to the school's application.) It was a mess.

The guys who drove the van were part of the bigger changes that were sweeping Black America during the 1960s. They were about four years older than I was, and able to see firsthand some of the pivotal moments in our recent history. They would have been old enough, for example, to travel to the March on

PART THREE

Washington in 1963 and hear Dr. King speak; feel the atmosphere in the street and talk to people after the Harlem riot during the summer of 1964; mourn the Audubon Ballroom shooting of Malcolm X in the winter of 1965; and shudder with foreboding in December 1966 when 400,000 young men were called up to fight in Vietnam. It began to dawn on me that these guys were my Prince Charming prospects.

I was already missing their company when the van pulled up to the Harlem church at the end of our trip and would think about my Prince Charming guys often. I'd see them at community events from time to time and learn of their triumphs and tragedies. Each earned a master's degree and became a successful professional. One became assistant pastor at one of Harlem's historic churches, and the other became a respected leader in education reform. One deceased at the age of 66; the other was widowed at 73 after cancer claimed the life of the college sweetheart, he had been married to for 50 years.

Shortly after his wife passed away, I saw a newspaper article about the guy who'd been widowed. As I read it, I was struck that, in addition to his professional accomplishments, commitment to community service, lifelong love of sports, and strong friendships, he had also been a steadfast life partner to his wife.

When I read the article, though, I felt a surge of compassion for my younger self and her appetite for sophistication and glamour. My younger self would not have been able to discern the difference between the swagger and dash of the Prince Charming of her imagination -- and the character and steadfastness of a Life Partner.

She would learn when she was much older that the ability to partner is not necessarily a Prince Charming virtue. She would also learn that partnering for life is, itself, a worthwhile path that

PART THREE

can guide even the shallowest heart toward a life of commitment, care, and devotion.

PART THREE

An Auld Lang Syne Salute to My New Year's Eve Marriage Proposals

With a tip of my hat to Robert Burns who, in 1788, said he got this song from an old man, I am reflecting this last day of the year on my three consecutive New Year's Eve marriage proposals. They came in 1982, 1983 and 1984, from three different potential partners. I was 34, 35 and 36, respectively, and my biological clock was ticking. I was obviously anxious about the whole clock thing and trying my best to snag someone before the shop closed for good.

The Scots words "auld lang syne" can be loosely translated into English as "long, long ago," or "for the sake of old times." The first line of the song asks the rhetorical question as to whether it is right for old times to be forgotten.

Should old acquaintance be forgot and never brought to mind?
Well, yes and no.

There is something magical about getting engaged on New Year's Eve. But it's fair to say that I may have overdone the thing. The first guy I was engaged to was the good friend of a guy I had known for many years. I'd met him at the mutual friend's September wedding and sized him up as a good prospect. He was an Ivy League graduate; I knew, liked, and respected many of his friends; and the chemistry was right. He moved into my apartment shortly after we met, and the future looked promising.

He proposed on New Year's Eve at a small gathering given by mutual friends, and I accepted his proposal. Our friends hugged and kissed us and offered their congratulations. The wedding was set for February 19. But, by the third week in January, a future with him didn't look so promising after all, and

PART THREE

I called off the wedding. My mother was thrilled; she never liked the guy anyway.

By the time I made the decision, though, I'd received our first wedding gift. It was a silver-plated serving platter from my mom's co-workers in the credit department at the now- defunct B. Altman's. I wanted to observe proper etiquette and return the gift. But because my mom's co-workers had chipped in to buy an item on which they were already getting the employee discount, they thought about the hassle of doing the math and said, "Nah, let her keep it." I still have and frequently use that silver-plated platter.

It would be the only "wedding gift" I'd ever receive.

Should old acquaintance be forgot and never brought to mind?

I met the second guy at one of the personal growth workshops I've always been fond of. He was very handsome, and, again, the chemistry was right. His family was from Trinidad; he was Catholic; and went to the same military boarding school that the exiled Nicaraguan dictator Anastacio Samoza's son attended while he was there. When I met him, he was developing a software business with an associate I didn't like. (I thought his business partner was a jerk.) Our relationship looked promising at first but lasted only six months.

We went to a formal dance on New Year's Eve, and I wore a long gown that billowed when I moved across the floor. The pièce de resistance was the crystal ball on the ceiling that twirled round and round, casting flecks of light on the ballroom floor. Everything was so romantic that night! He proposed to me under the twirling glass ball, and I accepted

By the time Good Friday came, though, I knew that marriage with him would never work, and told him about my feelings after the high mass we attended that day. Again, my mother was thrilled. "I always thought he was odd," she said.

PART THREE

Should old acquaintance be forgot and days of auld lang syne?
The third guy was my student in the same personal growth workshop where I had, by then, become faculty. He was a former pro-football player; had been raised Pentecostal; and worked in sales for a major computer company. He wanted very much to be married.

I knew from the start of our relationship that we were not a good match for each other. But on New Year's Eve, as we knelt to light candles after the midnight service at the Cathedral of St. John the Divine, he proposed, and I accepted.

Darn it, there I go again!

By mid-year, we both knew that getting married was not a good idea for us. This time, I didn't even bother to tell my mother. He'd soon be moving to Chicago, after all. There, he'd join a mega church and marry a woman who'd graduated from divinity school.

For auld lang syne, my dear, for auld lang syne.

By the light of day, I could see what I had been doing and took myself out of circulation." I'm hangin' up my toe shoes," I announced to myself. I realized that I knew *nothing* about relationships or marriage. And, as they say in another field, it was clear that I was "capable of doing harm to myself or others."

I was still young, though. Soon there would be the right guy for me, I told myself. And there would always be New Year's Eve, a night that portends a future that is a delightful mystery. It is full of possibility and -- if you're an optimist like me -- hope.

For auld lang syne, my dear, for auld lang syne We'll take a cup of kindness yet, for auld lang syne.

PART FOUR

PART FOUR

OUR INTIMATE CIRCLES OF CARING

PART FOUR

Thank You for Choosing Me

Being chosen is a big deal, and not being chosen is a big deal, too. We learn how we feel about both of these when we're kids and get picked or not picked to be on a team. We never forget the feeling. We are happy when we're chosen for a featured part in the school play, or when our best friend singles us out to share a backstage pass. We're unhappy when we don't get invited to a certain party, or when the college we want to go to doesn't accept us. Later, we're thrilled when the person we have the "hots" for chooses us, and we're hurt when they choose someone else.

As young people, we think of ourselves as being chosen or not chosen.

The other day, I went online to see what others might have to say about being chosen. I went there because I was deeply moved by the friend who had just thanked me for helping him with a problem and had said, "Thank you for choosing me." I wanted to marinate in the juiciness of the feeling that came over me. I wanted to savor the thought that my choosing had been important to him -- that I was important to him. It was in that moment that I began to consider that choosing might be just as big of a deal as being chosen.

It seems that by the time we're in kindergarten, we notice whether we're being chosen by others. Something in our make-up as human beings calls it to our attention. We want to be chosen because it makes us feel good. It makes us feel valued and worthy. We notice less how we feel when we do the choosing.

I'm thinking now of the story I recently heard about the little girl who told her mother that her best friend's dog had just died and that she wanted to go over to her friend's house right away. The mother didn't see the urgency in her daughter's need to go immediately and asked her what she could possibly do at her friend's house to help.

"I can go over there and cry with her," the little girl said without hesitation.

The little girl knew about choosing. She knew that her friend's loss was important and deserved to be shared with someone who cared. She knew that her friend's feelings mattered and that being with her would honor those feelings. Even as young children we know these things. We know about choosing.

While I was online, I read the writings of people who felt they had not been chosen. One wrote:

No one ever chose me. My mother chose her lovers, and my half-brothers. My Father chose the bottle. I chose (and chased) every lover I've ever had, and went after them like my life depended on making they choose me back. They didn't.

Another said:

It took years, huge embarrassments, broken friendships, and relationships for me to realize and own that I was always looking around for people to make me feel "chosen" because when my parents divorced and married other people, I felt abandoned and alone.

One of the writers said that not being chosen was like having a "wound" that never heals.

I want to say to the writers I saw online that not being chosen loses its sting as we get older. As my friends and I approach the age of 70, not being chosen looks different from the way it did when we were younger. When I asked one of my early-boomer friends whether he thought there was a difference between how we think now about being chosen and how we used to think about it, he said, "Hell yeah, it's different. We don't have the energy to think about that crap now!"

And I remember one of my friends saying that before she turned 50, she would walk into a room and wonder whether anyone there would like her. After turning 50, she said, when she walks into a room, she wonders whether *she'll* like anyone. It's different for us now, and being chosen means something different, too.

The revered psychologist, Abraham Maslow, said that at around the age of 55, we finally have a shot at being real grownups. His words are fancier than mine, but he identified certain markers for being what he called "a self-actualized person," including *post-ambivalence about our parents, enduring post-romantic love relationships, acceptance of the evil within ourselves, the courage to be openly virtuous, and peace with our mortality.*

If Life promises to give us all the goodies on Maslow's list, then hurray for Life! It doesn't work out that way for everyone, though, and some of us become "toxic agers" -- those for whom gratitude to Life is not in the cards.

In the late 1990s, a psychologist who did extensive research on toxic aging, wrote a book about how to cope with difficult elders, and warned us baby-boomers about becoming toxic as we age. Other experts on the subject talk about gratitude and gratefulness as keys to not becoming toxic. They talk about being thankful to life and appreciating the goodies that come with maturity. Indeed, the field of neuroscience now tells us that the older brain has a greater capacity for *thankfulness* than the younger brain.

Which brings me back to my theme:

I called one of my good friends to thank her for choosing me. She thanked me for choosing her, too. We meant it. We are grateful to have each other at a time when we're both
dealing with health challenges. We're grateful to have a committed listener who will help us sort through the twists and turns of life.

PART FOUR

I've known my good friend for about 20 years, and there are other friends I know from kindergarten, elementary school, high school, college, church, work, community life, my love life, and other chapters from my life. They chose to make me a part of their journey as they became spouses, divorced spouses, parents, professors, expatriates, grandparents, cancer survivors, retirees, stroke survivors, disabled, and more. I wouldn't be who I am today if I hadn't been chosen by them.

As my friends and I celebrate our seventh decade, being chosen looks different than it did back in the day. For many of us, being chosen means having witnesses to our growth and change. For others, being chosen means being accepted for who we are and who we are not. And for others, being chosen can mean being appreciated for our simple humanity.

Choosing also looks different to us and may now be as important as being chosen.

Choosing others gives us standing in life and says that we're doing our part to make sure our chosen ones feel grateful for being alive.

PART FOUR

Who Do You Belong To?

*H**ealthy humans need to be part of a group. That's how we survived throughout evolution, and that's how we survive today. Strong social relationships will affect not only your quality of life, but how long you live. Many of the social institutions that have supported humans throughout our history are rapidly changing, so we'll need to envision ways to successfully adapt.*

    This excerpt from *A Long Bright Future: Happiness, Health, and Financial Security in an Age of Increased Longevity,* by Laura L. Carstesen, Ph.D., hit me like a ton of bricks, and pointed me toward the tension I'd felt, but couldn't articulate during the past holiday season. It was the tension between *belonging* and *loneliness.* It was the friction I felt between no longer having close living family members with whom I always celebrated the holidays and the freedom I felt from the obligation to spend time with people I didn't especially want to be with.

    On one hand, I missed the intimacy that comes with belonging to a family. On the other, freedom from family obligations brought a feeling of loneliness. Fortunately, I knew that I was not alone in this regard. Holidays bring up the belonging-loneliness tension for many of us, and many of us are torn by it.

    Belonging is a big deal. It's right up there with other basic human needs and its fulfillment is essential to our well-being. The need to establish deep relationship bonds is so strong, psychologists say, that we are reluctant to dissolve even our most destructive bonds. Indeed, our sense of belonging is fundamental to our perceptions of having a good life.

PART FOUR

So, when I went to bed Christmas night and pulled up the covers, I said prayers of thanks for the church service I'd gone to with Eric that morning and for the dinner gathering I'd enjoyed with friends later in the day. It occurs to me as I write this now that I was grateful for belonging.

Some psychologists who write about belonging tell us that all human beings need a minimum quantity of regular, satisfying social interaction, and that the inability to meet this need can result in loneliness, mental distress, and -- in some cases -- physical illness.

A recent guru of such thinking was the late Dr. John Cacioppo, co-author of the book, *Loneliness: Human Nature and the Need for Social Connection*. Until his untimely death, he was an award-winning neuroscientist at the University of Chicago who pioneered the field of loneliness studies.

For Cacioppo, loneliness is the "painful feeling" that prompts human beings to reconnect to others. In an interview with a medical journal, Cacioppo said, "just like hunger and thirst and pain, loneliness signals something important for the survival of your genes -- the need for connection to other individuals."

Having studied loneliness for more than two decades, Cacioppo wrote that loneliness isn't necessarily the result of being alone. To be sure, bereaved spouses, deployed soldiers, and college freshmen can be around a lot of people and still feel deep isolation. For us humans, Cacioppo noted, *perceived isolation* is much more important than physical isolation.

A few days before Christmas, I read an article in *The New York Times* about how social isolation is "killing" us. It's a growing epidemic that is alarming health care providers. Further, the article says, the number of American adults who report being lonely has doubled from 20 percent to 40 percent since the 1980s. We are, as a society, lonelier than we've ever been.

The article also says:

Loneliness is an especially tricky problem because accepting and declaring our loneliness carries profound stigma. Admitting we're lonely can feel as if we're admitting we've failed in life's most fundamental domains: belonging, love, attachment. It attacks our basic instincts to save face and makes it hard to ask for help.

Loneliness for older adults -- and for those of us who will one day be older adults -- is not a singular phenomenon. It comes in many different forms. About a third of Americans over 65 live alone, and half of us who are over 85 do. Our potential isolation can lead to quality-of-life challenges that health care providers are only now associating with limited social connection.

For older adults who live in assisted living facilities, or who are institutionalized in nursing homes, loneliness and separation from our communities can contribute to deteriorating health. Those in poorer health or with mood disorders like anxiety or depression, are the least likely to have someone to talk to about important personal matters.

Here, I must acknowledge Laura Carstensen, the author I talked about earlier, and her insights about relationship-building for the older adults we baby-boomers are now becoming.

She devotes a section of her book to it and calls it, "Nourish Your Social Relationships."

Carstensen, the founding director of the Stanford University Center on Longevity, writes a lot about the impact that 30 extra years of life will have on the social structures we baby-boomers were born into. She tells us to brace ourselves for the unprecedented demographic shift we're now experiencing in which lifespan is increasing while birthrates are decreasing.

In the near future, Carstensen says, more generations in families will be alive at any one time than ever before; nuclear families will be smaller as more women decide not to have children; and marriage patterns will make the concept of family more fluid, with the possibility that a greater number of family members will be related by marriage than by blood.

We'll have to adapt, she says. As families become more fluid and less defined by blood ties, they could become less stable, and offer less social support than they used to. Part of our adapting in the 21st century will be to nurture relationships beyond kin. For, while we've inherited from our evolutionary past our intuition to bond with blood kin, the 21st century will call upon us to expand our domains of belonging and include people we'd never thought of before.

Carstensen writes:

Beloved family members die, children move far away. So, starting now, begin to diversify your "family" beyond your immediate biological ties and your relationship with your romantic partner. Create meaningful, reciprocal bonds with people who reflect different facets of your life -- friends, neighbors, colleagues, mentors. If you diversify, you are better insulated against unexpected changes that affect your network, such as illness, divorce, or relocation. The upside of creating "voluntary" families is that you have the opportunity to create social networks that include the people you like best. You don't have to lose the sister-in-law you adore just because she and your brother divorced. You can include your best friend in family celebrations, and get to know your best friend's family, too.

I'm reminded now of the story told to me by a friend who used to work for New York's Central Park and knew about its tree-planting program. It seems the park's gardeners were aware that planting a wide variety of tree specimen would protect the park from the harm of diseases that might wipe out a particular specie. They knew that plant diversity in the park would ensure both resilience and longevity. They knew that planting different kinds of trees would keep the park strong and beautiful for a long time.

PART FOUR

    I'm going to take a page out of their book today and diversify my "family." I want to be resilient like the trees in Central Park, and be strong and beautiful for a long time, too.

PART FOUR

The "Doing" of Intimacy

In my living room earlier this month, I began hosting a workshop called *The Way of the Wise Boudoir: Six Lessons on Intimacy and Mature Living*. I gathered a small group of women, and we looked at the areas in our lives where we have successfully developed intimacy and the areas where we would like to develop more of it.

We acknowledged that our mothers didn't – couldn't – tell us about the chapter of life we're living in now. Our moms were focused on the roles that society gave women back then, and we mature women today are thinking thoughts that weren't on our mothers' minds at all.

Indeed, my mother exhausted the roles she inherited: daughter, sister, wife, mother, aunt, worker, churchgoer, school volunteer, community advocate, care giver. When I -- her only child -- had no children, the role of grandmother remained a role she would never perform. If she'd had grandchildren, she might have lived longer than her 85 years. Who knows? I've often thought that she passed away when she did because there were no longer people in her family to take care of. It's as though "taking care" gave existential standing to women in the generations that preceded ours.

And now, some of us baby-boomers are grandmothers. We've performed all the roles that our mothers performed, but we're asking different questions of life and have different expectations than they did. Back in the day, we didn't associate "sexuality" – for example -- with being a grandmother. And now we do.

That's where having an intimate life comes into play. In our wise years, we start to think of intimacy as a domain that includes sex but involves much more than sex. We think of intimacy as something we do when we bond with our grandchildren or take care of a sick friend. Increasingly, we think of intimacy as the bond that develops between any caregiver and the one being cared for.

So, intimacy – whether it is sexual or emotional -- is about our capacity to bond. And as humans, we want to bond. We just don't always know how to do it.

Paul Taylor is the author of *The Next America: Boomers, Millennials and the Looming Generational Showdown*, a book that discusses how demographic trends are reshaping society today. He is also a senior fellow at the Pew Research Center, where he monitors emerging trends. I saw him in a cable TV interview where he defined the term "elderly orphans" as those baby-boomers, like me, who won't have younger family members around to care for us when we're older.

Taylor told his interviewer that the traditional family contract – *I'll take care of you when you're young and you'll take care of me when I'm old* – has been turned inside out by the decline in "family formation" that began with baby-boomers and continues with millennials.

The term, *elderly orphan*, caught me off guard as it did the women in the workshop when I told them about Taylor's book. After acknowledging that they either had no children, or that they had no expectation that their adult children would be caregivers for them, a few shared ideas about ensuring that they would have support in older adulthood. One said she had thought about living in a commune, another about buying a condo with friends and hiring a caregiver for the group.

PART FOUR

The traditional family contract has morphed, indeed, and it looks like we'll be bonding with non-family folks as we get older. Can we do so in a satisfying way, though? That's the question at hand. During the workshop, the members of our small group took a brief quiz and rated ourselves on our capacity to bond and be intimate with others. We gave ourselves homework assignments to challenge us in the areas where we had given ourselves low scores.

One area in which I gave myself a low score was my willingness to do things with others that I wouldn't do on my own. (I grew up as an only child. What do you expect?) When Eric invited me to do something with him, for example, I would always ask myself if it was something I'd choose to do anyway.

As soon as I saw my low score, I realized that not doing some of the things Eric wanted to do was intentional on my part. It was a behavior I'd adopted at the beginning of our relationship to maintain distance. I could see that this behavior of mine had been baked into our relationship like a permanent fixture.

So, for my homework, I watched Eminem's *8 Mile* music video with Eric. The point was not to tell him that I was doing my assignment, but to try something new that I wouldn't do on my own. He really wanted to show me the video and played it for me enthusiastically on his laptop. I'm not a fan of rap music, but I actually got into what Eminem had to say in *8 Mile* and I enjoyed sharing the new experience with Eric.

That was the learning for everyone in the group. We stepped out of our comfort zone and into a new experience. One group member did it with co-workers, another with an ex-lover, and another with her sister-in-law, and so on. Each of us stretched open a part of ourselves that was limited or closed and discovered that the person with whom we shared ourselves was delighted -- and grateful -- to bond with us.

PART FOUR

I'm seeing that we baby-boomers are going to need this capacity more and more as we make our way through the new possibilities for intimacy and bonding that lie ahead. Learning to open ourselves to one another in this way is going to be essential for our health, our happiness, and our humanity.

PART FOUR

Having a Close Circle of Intimates

They are my anchor, my intimates are.

I thought about this idea when I read the last chapter of Thomas Friedman's book, *Thank You for Being Late: An Optimist's Guide to Thriving in the Age of Accelerations*. I understood a phrase he used in that chapter -- "topsoil of trust' – as a metaphor for the suburban Minneapolis neighborhood where he grew up and learned the values that are still with him today.

I recalled, too, the walk-through I'd done more than a decade ago when I was consulting for a faith-based housing nonprofit in Brooklyn that renovates abandoned, city-owned buildings for low-income families. On a tour of the federally funded project our organization had just completed, one of the pastors who came with us on the tour noticed that there was not enough room in the model apartment for a kitchen table.

"So, where's the family supposed to sit down for dinner?" he asked.

He was saying, in so many words, that the small apartment didn't have enough space for a family to gather as a family. Obviously, the number-crunchers at the federal agency in Washington had given more thought to the economics of the project than to the intimate lives of the people who would live there

Intimacy is not a private thing; it's something we share with others. And as the world of technology accelerates at faster and faster speeds -- forcing us all to adapt, says Friedman -- we're going to need our circles of trust and intimacy to keep us grounded in our humanity.

PART FOUR

I was happy to hear about the book. I'm one of those early baby-boomers with a growing awareness that the accumulated wisdom of us older adults is not as valuable as we thought it would be. (The accumulated wisdom of our parents and grandparents seems to have worked out for them, though. It's as if new appliances had been installed in my kitchen overnight and I wasn't able to make breakfast in the morning the way I used to. The world we were born into isn't the world we live in now. And our bewilderment about it may be a sign that we're feeling "growing pains" at a time in life when we thought we'd be all grown up.

A couple of years ago, one of my friends sent me an iPhone for Christmas and I never learned about all the things it could do. I just wanted to make and receive phone calls. Last year, when I signed up for an in-home massage service, though, I learned that the company would only do business with me if I had a smartphone. Its business model was set up to connect with customers by text instead of by phone, and if I wanted to have a massage at home, I'd better get with their program and learn how to send texts.

And during the iPhone "tutorial" I had with my 20-something neighbor a few days later, I learned that I had to turn on the phone's GPS feature if I wanted to have an account with Uber. "No GPS," she said, "no Uber." So, like many baby-boomers, I'm still playing catch-up.

Friedman tells us that 2007 was the year when all hell broke loose, and the pace of change, itself, began to accelerate. That year saw the introduction of tech brands that are today's household names: iPhone, Twitter, Kindle, Airbnb, Android. And starting then, he says, Silicon Valley and tech researchers across the globe launched scientific and technological innovations – including "The Cloud" -- that speeded things up so fast that what used to change in a generation now changes in a couple of years.

PART FOUR

The other day, for example, I went to the eye doctor I've been seeing since the 1990s. I haven't seen him in a couple of years and learned that, since I'd last been to his office, the diagnostic technology for ophthalmologists had become so precise that he can walk past the open door of his examining room, glance quickly at the large desktop monitor that displays a magnified, digital image of my eyeball, and know what's going on with me before he walks into the room. He told me that when I became his patient 25 years ago, he would have had to darken the examining room, stand over me and look into my eye with a powerfully lit, high-magnification lens to see what computers can now see right away.

I remember, too, that when I was in high school there had been talk about a "cash-less society." At the time, I couldn't imagine how that would work. Today, not only are there electronic transfers of money and pre-paid debit cards, but we are now living in a world that is wireless, cordless and (coming soon) paperless.

Change is everywhere. And even when we can't see the changes with our eyes, we can feel them all around us. It's been dizzying, overwhelming, and anxiety-provoking for everyone, and for us baby-boomers, it's been a game-changer.

Baby-boomers have become digital *immigrants* in a world crafted by digital *natives*.

Indeed, we early baby-boomers were already in our mid-50s when the term, *digital native*, was first used. It refers to people born after 1980 who only know a world where computers, video games, and online activities are commonplace. Digital natives speak a language different from the one we early-boomers grew up with. As newcomers to their world, we must sound the way the foreign-born sound to us when they speak English with an accent.

Friedman wants his readers to understand that during this time of multiple accelerations we're all learning to "dance in a hurricane," and to find our personal sanctuary of stability inside the storm. Meteorologists call this place the "eye" of the hurricane. They know that the eye moves with the storm and draws energy from it. They also know that the "eye" of the storm is both dynamic and stable. So must we be, Friedman says.

Dancing in a hurricane is not a natural state for us human beings, he writes, and we're adapting to the challenge as fast as we can. To create the sanctuaries of stability that will enable us to "dance," Friedman sees us using the ancient wisdoms our ancestors used to cope with the big changes that confronted them. He sees us turning to our trusted ones -- as we've always done -- and reaching out to our communities of caring for reassurance.

Having circles of trust and intimacy has always been important to the human experience.

That's why tribes gathered around the fire at night, and its why families gather around the kitchen table. The campfire and the kitchen table are where we learn to build trust with our intimates. There, we can be vulnerable and unsure of ourselves. There, we learn that the circle will be there for us when change happens.

My close circle of intimates now includes the young people in my life who see the world differently than I do and assure me that the changes going on today are ones I'll eventually adapt to. They anchor me in the present in a way I didn't think I'd need at this stage of life. I don't feel obsolete – irrelevant – when I'm with them. Vulnerable and unsure, perhaps; obsolete, no.

Our children and grandchildren are helping us baby-boomers adapt to technological change and take social risks we'd never consider before. They are more inclusive of people who don't look like them and have learned not to think of their tribe as a closed domain. This thinking is new for us baby-boomers who thought the tribes we were born into would be around forever.

      We older adults are changing, to be sure. And through the eyes of the young ones who are in our lives, we are learning that close doesn't have to mean static, and intimate doesn't have to mean exclusive. We're learning that dancing in a hurricane is what everyone is doing now, and that our circle of intimates will be right there dancing with us.

PART FOUR

Seeing Intimacy through the Eyes of Intimacy

There is nothing more intimate than saying the final goodbye to our parents. It's a task that now befalls us babyboomers big time. It took me ten years to sort through my mother's personal effects, and I still haven't gone through all the boxes I brought home from my father's place. I'm an only child, so I'm grateful that there are no siblings waiting in the wings for the stuff they'd like to have.

We learn how to be intimate with others through practice with our parents and early caregivers. The grabbing, crawling, smiling, sucking, and drooling we do as infants are part of the "dance" we learn to do with them. It's amazing to consider that my ways of being intimate today began in that dance. It also amazes me that the belongings of the father whom I thought of as remote – not intimate -- spoke so generously and warmly to the men who helped me dismantle his apartment. It was as if my helpers were there to tell me things about my father that he could not share with his daughter.

Eric never met my father, but he worked with the guys to whom I assigned the emptying of closets and dressers and gave me insights about my relationship with my father that only a lover – another intimate – could offer. He was able to see similarities between father and daughter that were both subtle and profound.

"You're just like him," he said laughing. "I know," I said sheepishly.

There were four men on the task: Eric in his 60s; his Columbian friend, Jorge, in his 50s; my godson, Patrick, in his 40s; and Patrick's friend Otis, in his 30s. My father was six months shy

PART FOUR

of his 100th birthday when he died, so for Otis, the youngest man, the project was a history lesson.

As the men removed items from my father's closets and drawers, they marveled at the details of his life that the contents revealed. It was in comments from those men who had never met him (My godson, Patrick, was the only one who had known him) that I began to see a fullness that I hadn't seen before.

My parents separated when I was in kindergarten and legally divorced many years later after "no fault" divorce was introduced. He lived close to where my mother and I lived, so I spent a lot of time with him. And even though my mother, father, and I attended the same church, I didn't really know who my father was as a "guy."

The crew served me well. They took my father's measure as they sorted through his things. He had lived in his large studio apartment for more than 50 years and had accumulated a much. He was a neat freak and used his carpentry skills to make built-ins for storage. Carpenter. Musician. Composer. Soldier. Hunter. Photographer. Jeweler. Volunteer. Author. Athlete. Notary. Deacon. Retiree. Administrator. Small business owner. Graduate student. Community advocate.

That's what the crew saw. They were archaeologists, and his apartment was a site where the secrets of a lost kingdom were being exhumed.
Who was this guy?" Eric asked. "He was like a king who lived many lives."

My father was seriously old-school and had collected the accoutrements of gentlemanliness that have all but disappeared. Otis picked up a couple of tie clips from the chest on Dad's dresser, held them between his fingers, and asked with a wrinkled brow what they were.

"Oh, yeah," Eric said, "we used to wear them to hold our ties in place, but we don't use them anymore."

Everyone laughed.

The daughter was learning about her father through the eyes of men who had never met him, but who felt his spirit resonate through the walls of his home. I met Jorge and Otis for the first time that day, but they gave me glimpses of my father that I will treasure forever. Intimate moments can endure like that. There's magic in them.

Last week, a friend asked me why I was so passionate about intimacy. I didn't think about Jorge and Otis then, but now I can see that – when we are open to it – it's possible to have intimate moments with relative strangers.

Intimacy doesn't discriminate. It washes over the rich, the poor, people from uptown and people from downtown, those who are from the 'hood' and those who are not. It can wash over us when we're least expecting it and change us forever.

PART FOUR

Hearing Love from My Gran

"Who loved you?" This is the question that Florida psychologist, Nancy Davis, always asks her patients, according to *60 Minutes* correspondent, Lesley Stahl, in her book, *Becoming Grandma: The Joys and Science of the New Grandparenting*.

Stahl says that her conversation with Davis stood out from the other interviews she did for the book because of what Davis told her: "If nobody loved you in your first five or six years, you're screwed. There's a hole in you that never gets filled. It's like you can't know what love is unless somebody loves you during that time."

Stahl asked whether it was enough to answer, "My grandmother loved me," and Davis replied that it was. Indeed, Stahl had already concluded -- after all her interviews -- that a grandmother's love was like none other because it was "wholesome, consummate, and pure."

Every week, there are about 30,000 new grandparents in the U.S., and today some 60 percent of all grandparents are baby boomers. Our generation, born between 1946 and 1964, had its peak childbearing years between 1965 and 2004, and now our children have (or are having) children of their own. I'm one of those women who did not have children, so it's my friends' children – my goddaughters in a few cases -- who are now mothers.

The "New Grandparenting" that Stahl talks about is different from the old-school grandparenting we baby-boomers grew up with. Like most kids in our generation, I had parents and grandparents who had a lot in common. Theirs was a seamless continuity of social values and norms. All of them, for example, were from Florence, South Carolina where they had been schoolmates and neighbors. All were African American and had lived under legal segregation.

My mother's parents died in Florence when they were in their late 30s, so I had no living grandparents on my mother's side. Conversely, my father's parents, who had already gotten a divorce, moved to New York City as part of the Great Migration.

I called my paternal grandmother "Gran", and she was central to everything I did when I was a little kid. As her only grandchild, I didn't have to share her with anyone, and I liked it that way. I called my paternal grandfather "Pop" and I only saw him a few times a year before he passed away when I was in grade school. Gran, on the other hand, was in my life big time. Even after my parents separated, she remained steadfast in her grandparenting until her death when I was 16.

Stahl's book reminded me who Gran was as a grandparent: Before I was old enough to go to school, Gran would come to my mother's Harlem apartment every Thursday to play with me. Thursday, the unofficial "day off" for the black women, like my grandmother, who were "live-in help" in the homes of New York's wealthy white families. The family she worked for lived on

Manhattan's Upper East Side and owned a summer home in Westport, Connecticut.

When I was a preschooler, Gran was my caregiver during the summer, and took me to Westport to live with her. There, my playmate was Mary, the little white girl who lived next door, and Gran taught me as soon as she could that the rules for little white girls and little black girls were not the same. She taught me that although it was okay for Mary to come over to play in our yard, it was not okay for me to play in hers. I didn't understand why it was that way, but Gran told me to just obey her and not ask questions.

I liked spending time with Gran; she indulged me in ways my parents wouldn't. She listened to me talk for hours and hours as we rode the train from New York to Washington, DC to visit my father's younger brother, Uncle Phil. She waited patiently in toy departments as I picked out the toys, I wanted her to buy for me. "You're not the only pebble on the beach," she'd say when I got too full of myself, "there's a Little Rock in Arkansas." (Gran had a corny sense of humor.)

By the time I was eight, Gran had retired and moved to New Haven to live with her sister, and I spent every summer there with her until she died. She taught me so much. She taught me how to make the country remedies from Down South that are good for whatever ails you. She taught me new words, like how to "modulate" my voice. She taught me the way "colored" people were supposed to act around "white" people to avoid getting into trouble. She taught me how to pray.

My Gran loved me.

Today, grans love their grandchildren, too. The New Grandparenting has more to do with changes in society than it does with changes in love. Unlike a half-century ago when I was a kid, today's parents and grandparents don't necessarily share the same values. Indeed, today's grandparents may not even be blood kin to their grandchildren.

Stahl's book tells us that grandparents now reflect the cultural tides that are shaping the modern family. So, grandparents today are gay, lesbian, transgender, surrogate grans, step grans, grans whose children have children by *in vitro* fertilization or frozen eggs, and grans whose grandchildren have other grans from their partners' previous relationships.

PART FOUR

But the love part of grandparenting endures. Mother Nature sees to that, Stahl tells us. The "science" in the book's title refers to what we are learning from the field of neuroscience about how grandmothers "fall in love" with their grandbabies. It seems that the same brain circuitry that makes us fall head-over-heels in love with our sweethearts makes us fall irresistibly in love with our babies and grandbabies. Mother Nature bathes our brains in the hormone, oxytocin, also known as the "love hormone," and makes us bond *irresistibly* to those we love.

We can't help ourselves.

There was a time not that long ago when grandparents shared the same DNA, race, ethnicity, and social history as their grandchildren. We used to be able to see our grandchildren as an opportunity to continue the world we inhabited; we used to be able to perpetuate the "tribal thing" with our grandchildren as my grandmother did with me. It's harder for grandparents to do that now. Since 2000, the U.S. has become more racially, ethnically, and socially diverse, and my friends' children are having babies that challenge my friends' inherited urge to perpetuate the "tribal thing."

My grandmother lived in a binary world of black people and white people as did many of the black friends I grew up with. My friends' children, though, have spouses or partners who come from such diverse places as Sri Lanka, Russia, England, France, Korea, Austria, and Mexico. And they have made a new kind of "tribe" with their partners -- a new kind of family.

I'm seeing that even the most racially strident of my friends wants happiness for their children. They have opened their hearts to life's changes and fallen irresistibly in love with the babies their children have brought into the world. They have let Mother Nature guide them, and, not surprisingly, they are cherishing their grandbabies with all the love they have.

PART FOUR

Who would have imagined that love for a grandbaby could so powerfully change the way we see the world?

PART FOUR

Mystery and Intimacy

Last week, three of my friends lost their mothers, the first intimate most of us have. Each mother was between 90 and 100 years old, and each was a black woman. I was asked by one of my friends to write an obituary for her mother's funeral and found myself calling up memories of obituaries I'd read years earlier about my own mother's friends. It wasn't lost on me when I read the obits years ago, usually sitting next to my mom in a church pew somewhere, that these short bios never mentioned the deceased woman as having worked as a domestic, cook, or "day" worker. At the time, it struck me as odd to see that references to their work were always absent, even though I knew that the kind of work they did was the only work most black women were allowed to do when I was a kid.

To be sure, there were black women who were teachers, nurses, social workers, and secretaries, but most black women born 100 years ago did not have the luxury of an extended, formal education. Some black women were wives and mothers and did not work outside the home. Those who did, though, usually found themselves doing "black women's work." I knew my mother's and grandmother's friends through the years and knew that this was the kind of work they did. The obituaries printed in their funeral programs, therefore, did not want to remind us modern-day mourners of how the world of segregation was set up back then.

All this came back to me as I worked on the obituary I promised to write for my friend. I asked her and her siblings about their mother's work life, and they struggled for an answer. They remembered that, at some point, their mom had worked for the

PART FOUR

City of New York, but they weren't exactly sure what she did there.

I knew that I had asked the wrong question. Obituaries for black women who were born in the nineteen teens and 1920s don't have much to say about what they did for a living. For many of us baby-boomers who were born in the mid-20th century, that part of our mothers' lives will remain a mystery. Having a "job" back then was a novel thing for everybody, and most folks did what they could to get by. I'm thinking now that many of the things they did to get by are not the kinds of things they'd want to memorialize in an obituary. So, their obituaries speak, instead, of what they cared about, who they loved, and how they lived as Christians.

While I was thinking about what I was going to write in the obituary for my friend's mother, I came across a passage written by Liz Hill, a Soul Matters minister at All Souls Church, a Unitarian church here in New York, that shed new light on the subject for me:

When they read the eulogy about the person's life and accomplishments, that is just the "what" of their life. The thing people want to hear at a memorial service, the thing that brings comfort, stirs memories, invites tears and laughter, are the stories ... The stories become the "how" of a life, and that is how, over time, we remember the person who is gone.

The *"how" of a life.* That's the *mystery* our mothers and other intimates rarely tell us about. The "how" of our lives, for those of us who fall into the category the late Toni Morrison called "everybody else" are the ways we choose to navigate the currents of life. During an interview with TV journalist, Bill Moyers, Morrison famously said, "The Master Narrative is whatever ideological script is being imposed by the people in authority on *everybody else.*"

PART FOUR

So, the obituaries of black women who were born 100 years ago very much reflect how they dealt with the scripts that were imposed on them by the *people in authority*. Some even crafted mysteries about who they really were.

I'm thinking now of my mother's good friend from church who sometimes "passed" for white to get work. She had been my Sunday school teacher, so I knew that she was very fair-skinned and made nothing of it. One day, in the late 1950s, when my mother and I were shopping downtown, we went into a Chock-Full O' Nuts, the New York City-based chain of lunch counters that served coffee and sandwiches and saw my mother's friend working as a waitress behind the counter.

Waitressing in a downtown coffee shop was not something black women did in those days, so my mother whispered softly (but with firmness) into my ear and told me not to speak to her friend. The people who worked at Chock Full O' Nuts, my mother later explained, might not know that her friend is a "Negro," and we didn't want to make trouble for her. So, Mommy and I sat down at the counter, ate our sandwiches, and pretended that we'd never seen her friend before. We pretended not to know her, and her friend pretended not to know us.

In the Master Narrative that then prevailed, a black mother and her daughter would have had no reason to be friends with a white waitress.

Life was like that back then. And there were countless black families who falsified their name, address, lineage, income, place of origin, marital status, level of education, and more to navigate the currents of life. These were some of the hoops one had to jump through when the people in authority-imposed scripts that made living with integrity nearly impossible.

Black people were not the only ones to craft mysteries, though. History is full of stories about how the famous and the not-so-famous "made up" accounts of who or what they were to satisfy the scripts imposed by the people in authority.

In William Shakespeare's London, for example, it was a no-no to be Catholic, so the playwright concealed his Catholic baptism, and lived publicly as a Protestant. Today, there is a thriving, illegal market in the U.S. for the "official" papers needed by undocumented immigrants to secure work, housing, schooling, a driver's license, and other basic necessities of life.

Yesterday, I saw a story on TV about a male-to-female transgender Filipino who had sex reassignment surgery in Thailand, and who now lives as an international supermodel in Europe.

Each person will remain a mystery to many because of the "how" of their lives. Each may have a time and place where they divulge their mystery to an intimate.

Or not.

Many mothers never divulge their mysteries to their children because the mysteries are too grim and their struggles too painful. I'm thinking now of the title character in William Styron's novel, Sophie's Choice, and her heart-rending decision to choose which one of her two children would go to the Nazi gas chamber. In Beloved, Toni Morrison's character, Sethe, kills her two-year-old daughter to make sure her child won't be captured into slavery. These stories are from fiction, but our real-life mothers had their stories, too.

What might be the stories our mothers never told us? What might be their mysteries? We loved them without knowing the "how" of their lives and without knowing their mysteries.

They loved us, too, even as they navigated the currents of life.

When they're gone, we'll be weaving our own stories about them, and holding them in memory in our carefully woven

PART FOUR

way. And even if we never know the "how" of her life, we'll forever feel the love our first intimate held for us in her heart.

In the end, that'll have to be full enough and rich enough for ours.

PART FOUR

Intimacy as Life's Agenda

End-of-year holidays are a time when our relationship with intimacy hits us in the face. During other times of the year, we can let our relationship with intimacy simmer unattended on autopilot and go about our daily lives leaving intimacy tucked away in the background.

During the holidays, though, intimacy is very much in the foreground. We are reminded at every turn that intimate relationships matter. The seasonal songs piped into malls and elevators remind us. The commercials on TV remind us. The friends and acquaintances who ask who we'll be spending the holidays with remind us. Our childhood memories remind us.

We are unavoidably directed to our relationship with intimacy during holiday time. We may even find ourselves reflecting on our relationship with "relationship" itself. The self-consciousness of it all is staggering and provokes stress for many of us. All families experience tension to some degree, and part of the reason holidays can be so stressful is the unrealistic expectation of coming together as a happy family. (The Norman Rockwell 1942 painting of the happy family sitting down for a turkey dinner haunts us all.)

Our stress response to the holidays is so widespread that a well-known stress-diagnostic protocol pre-printed Christmas on the list with other life events that cause elevated stress levels. Working in the mid-1960s, psychiatrists Thomas Holmes and Richard Rahe researched the link between stress and illness and came up with a list of 41 life events and their corresponding stress levels. Known as the Holmes and Rahe Scale, it has since then served as a tool for identifying risks for stress-related illnesses.

PART FOUR

I first saw the list in the 1970s and was surprised to see Christmas pre-printed on it. It seems that whether we celebrate the holiday, we are subject to the anxieties that come with the season. When I looked at the list recently, I noticed that the five life events that rank highest on the stress scale also put our relationship with intimacy at risk: death of a spouse, death of a close family member, divorce, marital separation, and imprisonment. It appears that our health is threatened when our prospects for intimacy are diminished.

I looked at the next eight life events, and saw the same connection to intimacy: marriage, dismissal from work, marital reconciliation, retirement, dramatic change in the health of a family member, pregnancy, sexual difficulties, and gaining a new family member. It seems that our health and well-being exist in sympathy with the health and well-being of our circles of caring.

I learned how important circles of caring can be when I worked at a small nonprofit in the 1990s. It was an intimate office with fewer than ten people on staff. I was a proposal writer who, for a short time, shared a cubicle with our part-time accountant. She and I had had an argument in the fall (I forget what it was about) and were not on speaking terms when the annual Christmas party was being planned.

As fate would have it, I picked her name from a hat to be my "Santa Pal" and struggled all day with the idea of swapping her name for someone else's. I took a long bus ride that afternoon and found myself chatting with the bus driver about my dilemma. I don't recall what he said, but I decided to keep her as my Santa Pal, and buy her a gift.

Our office mates thought of the accountant as a well-dressed, very feminine, wife and mother who had champagne tastes. I didn't know her very well, so I took my cue from them, bought her a glittering perfume atomizer for her vanity and wrapped it as beautifully as I could. When I presented it to her at our Christmas party, she opened it with a smile, gave me a big hug, and thanked me for it. Our co-workers enthusiastically agreed that the gift matched her style.

    When our boss called me into his office after the party was over, he told me that my Santa Pal gift had made our small office a family again. He said that the feud between the accountant and me had put lots of tension into the air in the office, and that our gestures of good will had cleared the air for everyone. He told me that the accountant and I were professionals who were respected by the staff, and that our feud was inconsistent with what others in the office thought of us. He also told me that the accountant and I were very much alike, and that if I got to know her, I would like her.

    I never forgot that moment. I learned that I was part of a circle of caring whether I was conscious of it or not. I hadn't thought of my workplace as a domain for intimacy, but what I learned from my boss that day taught me that it was.

    Many years later, I learned that although I'll never see myself the way another sees me, life gives us intimates who can "read the tea leaves" for us and help us find our way through the maze of day-to-day living. Without our intimates, we can stumble unnecessarily and remain blind to what's going on around us.

    Our relationship with intimacy needs tending, though. I guess we should be grateful that every year during the holiday season, life puts intimacy on the agenda and directs us to take care of it.

PART FOUR

A Harlem Christmas Memory

I just re-read Truman Capote's 1956 short story, *A Christmas Memory,* and was struck by the phrase he used to capture the intimacy of the special friendship he enjoyed as a little boy with an adult cousin. At the end of the story, Capote refers to her as "an irreplaceable part of myself."

On this Christmas Eve, I'm thinking about two adults from my childhood who did as much to shape the inner landscape of my young life as my mother and father did. Like Capote's cousin, Mildred Johnson and Rev. James Robinson are "irreplaceable" parts of myself, and my Christmas memories of them today rush into the deepest crevices of my being.

I grew up in Harlem in the 1950s and 1960s, and attended The Modern School, the private school in the Sugar Hill area of Harlem that Mildred Johnson founded in 1934. I also attended the Church of the Master, the Presbyterian church, close to my home in Central Harlem that Rev. Robinson founded in 1939. In the same way that parents "drop off" their kids at school, the two of them "dropped off" this little girl for an expanded experience of *life.*

Mildred and Rev. Robinson were worldly and cosmopolitan in ways that a legally- segregated society did not contemplate for black people. Each modeled for me a way to craft a life that could triumph over the narrow domains assigned to black people.

Mildred Johnson (who insisted that her students call her "Mildred") was the daughter of J. Rosamond Johnson and niece of James Weldon Johnson. The two brothers were architects of the Harlem Renaissance and authors/composers of *Lift Ev'ry*

Voice and Sing, known also as the Negro National Anthem. Her father and uncle had been successful composers and songwriters for the Broadway stage during the early years of the 20th century, and her uncle had served in diplomatic posts under President Theodore Roosevelt. Mildred was about as close to being Harlem royalty as a person could get!

Her "Uncle Jim" (James Weldon) had also been a board member of the New York Society for Ethical Culture, a multi-racial, social justice organization that was founded in 1877. The Society had been an incubator for such progressive causes as the settlement house movement, the ACLU, and the NAACP, and had established a school here in New York City that pioneered progressive education.

Mildred attended the school -- Ethical Culture -- from her first day of kindergarten until her graduation from and certification by its Teacher Training Institute. She brought the tenets of the progressive education she'd been exposed to and the values of the Ethical Culture Society to Harlem in 1934 when she opened the doors of The Modern School.

I went to The Modern School from my first day of kindergarten until my graduation from eighth grade and would be immersed in Mildred's world for my entire childhood. In summer, I'd go to Dunroven Camp, the sleep-away camp she operated in the Catskill Mountains, and learned there how to swim, ride a horse, and hit a softball. Later, as an adult, when I joined Mildred and other old-timers on the school's Board of Directors, I still believed that black children deserved the expansive thinking, rigor and support the school offered.

It was Mildred's idea, for example, to enroll three of us six graders in a summer demonstration project at Teachers College in 1960 where, for the first time, we'd be in class with white students. I still don't know what the graduate students at TC where

PART FOUR

investigating, but I think it had something to do with engaging high-performing middle-school students in college-level academic material in a college setting.

Our studies that summer focused on the Italian Renaissance, and I was assigned to do research and write a paper about the Florentine painter, Sandro Botticelli. Our class made several field trips to the Metropolitan Museum of Art to view works by Renaissance painters and Botticelli had become my favorite. I felt so mature when I later applied to college and had no fear of being overwhelmed by the new environment. I'd already been there!

Mildred was big on culture. Each Friday, the school had an assembly program where every class had to perform a song, poem, skit, or presentation of some kind. And twice a year, Mildred staged a "festival" for which she was always the principal writer, director, and choreographer. She staged all these festivals at the Audubon Ballroom in Harlem, so it was a poignant moment for me when, less than a decade after my last festival there, the Audubon Ballroom became known to the world as the place where Malcom X was assassinated.

For one of her Christmas festivals, Mildred cast me to sing a solo. The song she picked was *The Christmas Song*. My whole family had fallen in love with the Nat King Cole hit, so I knew the song pretty well: *Chestnuts roasting on an open fire. Jack Frost nipping at your nose.* The costume my mother put together for me was amazing. She made a beautiful red velvet dress (she was a dressmaker by training) and bought white rabbit accessories – muff, ascot, and headband – to complete the outfit. When I tried everything on, it looked so great that I didn't want to take it off!

My moment alone on stage in my red and white outfit was magical and made me feel like a movie star. With the spotlight following me across the stage as I sang my song, trying my best to remember all the steps Mildred had taught me, I felt that life couldn't get any better than that. I silently wished that I could bottle the day and save it forever.

I wanted to make Mildred and my mother proud of me. Working with Mildred on the steps to my song and standing as still as I possibly could for my mother during the fittings, I knew that something important was happening. Maybe that something was love.

Thank you, Mildred, for this precious Christmas memory.

At school, Mildred's annual Christmas festival was where we students could perform for parents and friends. At church, Rev. Robinson's annual candlelight service was where the church's choirs could sing the season's sacred music for members of the congregation and their guests. At school, I became intimate with the optimism of Christmas, at church, with its awe.

Unlike Mildred, Rev. Robinson hadn't grown up in Harlem. He grew up in the "Bottoms" of Knoxville, Tennessee and in Cleveland, Ohio. The grandson of people who had been enslaved, he attended Lincoln University, an historically black college in Oxford, Pennsylvania, where he was classmates with Kwame Nkrumah, the man who would later become Ghana's first president.

After graduating from college, Robinson attended Union Theological Seminary in New York where he earned his degree in divinity. In 1938, with support from the leading Presbyterian clergyman who headed the denomination in New York City, he founded The Church of the Master in Harlem. It would be the first Presbyterian church in the city to have a predominantly black congregation.

As a pastor in impoverished World War II Harlem, Robinson introduced several progressive community development initiatives, including two summer camps for Harlem children in New Hampshire, where a multi-racial team of New England college volunteers built and staffed the sites. Later, when he traveled to Africa as a representative of the Presbyterian Church, he saw the challenges that faced the continent's newly emerging nations and determined that the multi-racial, college-volunteer model he used in Harlem could help build infrastructure in African communities, too.

In 1958, he founded Operation Crossroads Africa and traveled with a group of 60 people to five countries in West Africa to help build schools, churches, and libraries. Crossroads Africa soon became America's premier cross-cultural exchange program, and, by 1962, had been dubbed by President John F. Kennedy as the "progenitor" of the Peace Corps.

The year, 1958, was also when I started going to Sunday school at Church of the Master and attending Sunday morning services there with my mother. I was 10 years old. The church would soon become our family's church, though, for despite my parents' separation when I was five years old, my father had already joined the choir there and we'd see him every Sunday.

Years later, my mother and my father became church officers, and I, too, sang the choir.

Soon after I started going to the church, I could see that, like Mildred, Rev. Robinson was expanding my exposure to the world. Each spring, for example, our Sunday school would visit a nearby synagogue for a special Passover *seder* for children and learn to sing songs in Hebrew that Jewish children had learned. Each summer and fall, the church would host the white college students from New England who had volunteered for Crossroads Africa, and young people like me could hear them talk, not only about the countries in Africa where they'd worked during the summer, but also about the colleges they'd be attending in the fall.

PART FOUR

And each December, the congregation would be regaled by the baroque music we heard at the annual Candlelight Service.

I went with my mother to my first Candlelight Service the year we started going to the church and was wonderstruck by grandeur of it all. Green garlands draped the walls of the sanctuary and lush velvet bows were mounted at the ends of each pew. Red poinsettias were arranged along the edge of the pulpit and a bright red carpet had been rolled down the center aisle. The church was beautiful beyond words.

The choir sang the Christmas section of Handel's Messiah, and the accompaniment that evening included brass, strings, and tympani. The music lifted me up and took me to a place where, if I closed my eyes, I could see gold glittering everywhere. Then, before we all sang the Hallelujah Chorus, the lights in the sanctuary were dimmed, and, one-by-one, we lit our candles and illuminated the hall again.

"And He shall reign forever and forever," we sang raising our candles.

The sacred and the secular intertwined that evening. It was 1958, and it was unusual in Harlem to see black people and white people in the same church. It was also unusual for me to see my mother and father in the same room.

Thank you, Rev. Robinson, for bringing people together. And thank you for this precious Christmas memory.

PART FOUR

A Love Letter to Kendi

Last night I dreamed that the pandemic was finally over, that we could all go back to the lives we used to lead. When I jumped out of my sleep at 3 a.m., though, I found myself reaching for the blanket I keep at the foot of the bed. I was cold; I felt sad and anxious. In my dream, I'd seen a large crowd of unmasked faces, noses, and mouths, but couldn't spot a single smile among them. No one looked happy.

Kendi, when you and I said goodbye to our day jobs a few years back, we so looked forward to spending more time with family and friends, to enjoying retirement. I'm afraid that, with all the Covid-required social distancing and remote gatherings going on, we've forgotten how to relish life.

I started writing the Wise Boudoir blog ten years ago when we baby-boomers first learned that our life expectancy was going to be considerably longer than we'd thought that we'd have a lot more time to hang out with each other and have fun. Some longevity experts were even predicting that many of us would live to be 100! I wanted to tell the world that these experts were delighted about our new expected durability, that they were pumping up the idea that the more intimacy we have in our lives as older adults, the healthier and happier we'll be.

I also wanted to write about the ideas emerging from the fields of brain science, human sexuality, gender studies and evolutionary biology, asserting that human beings -- at all ages – need close, intimate relationships in order to thrive, both physically and emotionally. When we don't have those, we're warned, we'll be risking all kinds of threats to our well-being. I wanted my readers to know, too, what today's thought leaders had to say about aging, loneliness, disability, our widening range of sexualities, and so much more.

But when I went "live" with the blog, I immediately noticed the absence of other writers including intimacy in their discussions about older adults. I was puzzled. When talking with folks our age, I'd always heard all about the longings and frustrations of people who wanted to find their special person or make the relationship they already had a better one. Knowing that there was this strong yearning among us for satisfying connections, I thought there would surely be lots of voices online who were speaking our language.

I couldn't have been more surprised, then, to see that my Wise Boudoir was alone, the only voice, the singular voice I could find on the web exploring how we older adults were gettin' down hot and steamy with each other and crafting new ways to enjoy intimacy.

Remember the post I wrote about my 70-something friend who met the 70-something knee surgeon at the medical conference she was staffing? How he'd invited her to have dinner with him at the end of the conference, and how they'd spent a fabulous night together in his hotel room? And remember that she called the next day to tell me what a great time they'd had, and how flummoxed she'd been about the pleasure and joy that was still galloping around in her body the morning after?

Well, experts argue that enjoying moments like these is one of the intimate things we older adults can do with, and for, each other. But Kendi, I'm not sure that after years of living with this terrifying and ubiquitous virus that has dictated apartness, we'll ever be open to having spur-of-the-moment romps like that again.

That said, I did hear a great story some time ago that gave me hope about the future of intimacy for us older adults. A couple in their mid-90s, who'd been married for more than 60 years, were still enjoying pleasuring each other. They'd told James, the young man on the caregiving team that visited them every week, that they wanted to have more intimacy, and asked if he knew of something they could do about it. (That's not exactly the whole truth, though. It was actually the husband who'd initiated the whole thing.)

The husband told James about the post-surgical "device" his doctor had set up that was limiting intimacy with his wife. It seems that the surgeon who'd performed the procedure had attached a colostomy bag to the husband's abdomen at the end of the operation, and that the bag was such a turn-off for his wife that she didn't want to go anywhere near it.

James, the caregiver, was a good friend of mine. He'd been following the blog for years and wanted to talk with me about the couple in light of some of the challenges I'd written about. One of the posts I discussed with him was about endorphins, the hormones produced in our bodies which function to decrease pain and boost pleasure.

Each one of us releases endorphins into our bloodstream when we do a host of pleasurable activities: eat dark chocolate, exercise, have sex, dance, sing, laugh with friends, have a massage, gossip, ride a roller coaster, take a hot bath, and much, much more. The good news is that when we release endorphins, we feel great: we feel the euphoria of having great sex combined with the happiness of having Santa bring everything on our Christmas lists.

In my post about endorphins, I said that one of the best things about them is that we continue to produce and release these feel-good hormones, still as fresh as ever, no matter how old we are. I told James that if the couple were open to making their bodies feel great, learning how to release endorphins for each other might be a perfect solution for them.

PART FOUR

Wanting to learn as much as I could about my own endorphins, I experimented with a few of the activities that are known to release them. I became a human guinea pig for a while, and Eric, always ready to try something new, joined me in the adventure. Our favorite activities turned out to be giving each other massages, "making out" like young teenagers, laughing at old sitcoms, and chair dancing (you know that both Eric and I have mobility issues, so we sat on the barstools at my kitchen counter, listened to our favorite jams and chair danced to our hearts' delight). We had so much fun! Over time, James was able to introduce the 90-something couple to the wonder of their endorphins and encourage them to enjoy the feelings that swept over their bodies when the hormones were released. And even though the husband had previously told his caregiver that it was old-school sex with his wife he wanted, he learned that having so many different ways to experience pleasure with her -- and to make her feel great, too – was making him a very happy guy.

The couple eventually decided to take the bold step of experimenting with ways to give each other satisfaction. It was a new activity for them; they felt as vulnerable and shy about it as old-school newlyweds on their wedding night. Nervously and timidly, they began to tease each other about what they called their "endorphin-releasing-dates," and discovered new ways to "wow" each other with delightfully erotic sensations. The bag problem quietly disappeared.

Kendi, for me, this couple's journey is a snapshot of how I'd like to be in my nineties: open to new possibilities, intimately engaged with others (perhaps still in a relationship with Eric) and established in the kind of networks of support they had. I started the blog because I, too, want to win at being an older adult. Because I want to enjoy my sexuality as long as I'm able.

PART FOUR

Older adulthood today is different from the one you and I inherited from our parents. The version they knew didn't have online dating, fluid sexual identities, pleasuring for its own sake, sex toys, and the social goings-on that burst onto the scene in our lifetime. Our parents' life-expectancy was shorter than ours will be; it was impossible for them to teach us "the ropes" about being older adults.

It's gonna be up to our generation, then, to chart ways of navigating this new life-stage. There's been some public attention (not nearly enough) about providing basic needs for older adults: healthcare, affordable housing, nutritious food, support services, and social activities, amongst others. But little attention has been given to intimacy and the ways to embrace it as a permanent priority in our lives. The thought leaders I've been writing about have great ideas about caring for our emotional and relational needs, but their work is mostly tucked away in the silos of academia, and certainly not part of everyday conversation.

The underreported "loneliness epidemic" among older adults that was diagnosed more than a decade ago speaks volumes about how silent our society has been when it comes to intimacy. Made worse by the isolation imposed by the pandemic, our loneliness and longing for human connection led us to rely more and more on social media during the lockdowns, exposing ourselves, as a result, to online scammers who were targeting our solitude. According to the U.S. Federal Trade Commission, online romance scams in 2020 for folks our age increased by 65% over 2019, bilking us for more than $80 million! Grandparent scams weren't far behind the romance scams, with bad guys contacting us with tall tales about grandchildren who had just been arrested (don't tell their parents, they'd warn) or kidnapped, even, and needed money from us right away to bail them out or be released.

PART FOUR

During the shutdown, our loneliness, isolation, and marginalization became low-hanging fruit for predators -- both virtual and real-life -- while our deep needs for human touch and intimate connection remained unmet.

I see now how fortunate I was to be in a long relationship with Eric when I started writing the blog. I got so much energy from the groove he and I had carved out for ourselves that I was able to carry its comfort and security with me wherever I went. I'm not sure I'd have been able to dive as deeply into intimacy as I did if Eric hadn't been in my life.

And you, Kendi. I can't imagine life without our friendship. As you can see, I'm still struggling with my anxieties about the virus, and worrying how folks our age are gonna bounce back when things get back to normal. We'll still need each other to get through the twists and turns of older adulthood, won't we? None of us should try to do this thing alone.

Love always,
Liv

PART FIVE

SEXUALITY AND DISABILITY

PART FIVE

Learning to Be Sexy on One Leg

I picked up my walker from the doctor's office last week, and Eric went there with me. I was happy to feel the sturdy support of the U-Step Stabilizer, a mobility device especially designed for people with MS and Parkinson's, but even happier to feel Eric's support and hear him say "mushy" things to me during the medical adventure. Afterwards, we came back to my apartment and hung out for hours laughing, talking, and munching on cool summer fruits.

When I saw my physical therapist the next day, he asked how I felt about using the walker. I told him that walking with it made me feel more upbeat. It allows me to stand taller, and walk with more confidence, I said. He told me that he was relieved that I had finally gotten it and said that many of his patients refused to use a walker because they didn't want others to see them as disabled.

"That's why I wanted to have my boyfriend with me when I picked it up," I admitted. "He even said "boyfriend things" to me while we sat in the doctor's waiting room."

"Good for you," said the therapist laughing. "That's what I like to hear."

I've written about it before: Those of us who are older adults, or who have physical limitations don't always think of ourselves as sexually attractive. On the day I picked up my walker, it was important to not only feel attractive, but to have Eric there with me and feel that I was also attractive to him.

"Who'd have me? I have nothing to offer," said a man on one of the MS support phone calls I participated in.

PART FIVE

"I'll think about having a social life after I've lost 15 pounds," a friend told me.

Another friend who is a cancer survivor acknowledged that he now feels like "damaged goods."

If using a walker can make us feel less attractive, or dampen our sex appeal, it makes sense that many of my therapist's patients would refuse to use one.

I'm reminded, though, of sexy Blair Underwood -- and before him Raymond Burr -- playing the TV character Detective Chief Ironside who was big-time-sexy in his wheelchair. I'm also reminded of an interview I recently saw on Book TV with the author of a new biography of diplomat-politician-editor-playwright Claire Boothe Luce who was big-time-sexy until the end of her long, illustrious life.

In the old days, Luce would have been called a "vamp," the author tells us. It seems that, as the celebration party for her 80th birthday was winding down, the still sexually magnetic Luce was seen stroking the beard of the younger man she was sitting alone with on her sofa. The man later told the author that for the first time in his life he had come close to being romantically seduced by an 80-year-old woman.

Ah, seduction.

The good news is that we can all seduce whether we're in our 20s or our 80s. As humans, seduction is in our DNA. It's an onramp that invites others to have fun with us. It announces that we are a possibility for something wonderful to happen.

This is true whether we use a walker or not. The user manual that came with my walker did not require that I relinquish my ability to seduce in order to use it. If that trade-off should be in the cards in the future, I can say right now, "No, I'll never make that trade-off."

PART FIVE

Seducing is one of the super-powers given to us humans when we come into the world, and we learn to seduce when we're still babies. We smile, laugh, giggle, grab and let our parents and other caregivers know that we want to engage them.

Later, we join our friends in playful games that excite our desire to bond with others. And even later, as teens, we practice different kinds of seduction to glimpse the possibility of a romantic connection. By the time we're mature adults, then, we've been seducing others for most of our lives. We may even be experts at it, and not even know it.

Seduction is a powerful thing, to be sure. It creates the magnetic field that draws to us the people we want to be close to. And should the day dawn when I have only one leg, I'll still want to be close to other people and ask some of them to dance with me.

PART FIVE

Chair Dancing and the "Big Boss Turn"

It's not the sultry chair dancing Beyoncé did to open the Grammy Awards some time ago.

If you want to chair dance like Beyoncé, reported *Elle.com* in its online feed during the show, you have to wear a super-sexy dominatrix outfit with your hair in a wet-look; sit on a chair with your legs spread far apart; keep an intimidating look on your face; drape your legs over the top of the chair, bringing both legs together and swinging them from side to side; lie down on the chair with your face up, smiling just a bit; and then snap up, walk away from the chair, and never look back.

After watching her chair dance to *Drunk in Love*, a tuxedoed-and-bow-tied Jay-Z strutted from the wings onto the Grammy stage to join his wife in the steamy, sexually explicit song. The international power couple then lit up TV screens across the globe with provocative moves that could stimulate even the driest libido.

It's not that kind of chair dancing.

And it's not the chair dancing of the fitness gurus who promise improved muscle tone, flexibility, and cardiovascular endurance. At *chairdancing.com*, one reads that this fitness activity offers the fun of a dance exercise, the benefits of no-impact aerobics, and the convenience of a rigorous workout that can be done anywhere, in any shoes, in any clothing, on any floor surface.

It's not that kind of chair dancing, either.

And it's not the chair dancing people do at their computers while they're at work or do while they listen to music on their cell phones. I just read an entry in the *Urban Dictionary* that some chair dancers are listening to *cellcerts* -- a new word for reputation on the dance scene), and they have logged many hours together at the backgammon table. Indeed, Eric swears he taught her how to play the game. (I'm staying out of that one!)

The inspiration I saw in her swag became even more personal when I, too, was diagnosed with MS a few years ago. Such late-life diagnoses are rare, and I'd been using a cane for months without knowing what was causing the weakness in my right leg. When my doctor told me that it was MS, I pictured my friend on her scooter at a casino in Monte Carlo kickin' ass big time!

Swag seems to be good for your health. It keeps you vital, fresh, desirable, and sexy. I beg all my friends who are older adults to hold on to their swag. Keep tabs on it, I say. Check yourself out when you pass a mirror to make sure it's still there with you.

It may sound like an oxymoron to put the words "older adult" and "swag" in the same sentence. But think about it. If there's one thing worth being vigilant about as we get older it is not losing our personal power. Well, that's what swag is: Personal Power. I'm feeling now that I might be asking for trouble when I put "personal power" and "older adult" in the same sentence. It's almost as transgressive as saying that disabled people want to have "thrills" in life like everybody else does.

Eric and I fight a lot and make up a lot. When we made up last time, we sat looking out at Central Park, and talked about how we're similar and how we're different. For the first time, I told Eric how much I admired and loved his swag. He told me that he loved mine, too.

In that conversation, we made a new kind of pledge. We pledged to help one another to keep our swag – our aliveness, our uniqueness. I told him that he could count on me, and he told me that I could count on him.

PART FIVE

At 65, it's exciting to know that there is someone in the world who admires your swag and wants to help you to keep it.

anxiety. Some have self-defeating thoughts, she says, in which they believe that others are having great sex that they can't have, that no one wants to be bothered with them, or that they are not worthy of desire. Socially, there is the risk of self-isolation, or the shame, anger, and resentment of not being able to keep up with friends.

Boyle reassures, though. "Take control," she says. "Embrace the changes. Know your own body. Remain flexible. Be open."

For people whose prescription medications diminish sexual response, for example, taking control can mean asking health care providers to look for alternative treatments. This strategy can be especially helpful for users of medications that treat depression and hypertension but lower the libido.

For the 65-year-old woman whose vaginal dryness made sex painful, embracing the changes that were happening in her body meant securing prescriptions from her female urologist for a Viagra gel for her clitoris and Valium suppositories for her vagina.

For Boyle, knowing your own body means "body mapping." She urges people to take the time to touch every part of their body and gain greater familiarity with each part. See what feels the same and what feels different since you were diagnosed, she says. If the disability has resulted in oversensitivity in one area of the body, then explore new avenues for pleasure and new erogenous zones.

For the husband who had tried Viagra, Cialis, and Levitra, being flexible meant trying the vacuum pressure pump that rushes blood to the spongy tissue of the penis to make it erect. As long as the pump's band stays at the base of his penis, he will stay hard.

For the disabled man who called during the Q&A session, being open meant trying anal stimulation of the prostate to induce

PART FIVE

Sexuality and Disability

A few weeks ago, I listened in on a teleconference sponsored by the National Multiple Sclerosis Society. It was called *MS, Sex, and Intimacy*. The facilitator, Pamela Boyle, has been working in the field of sexuality and disability for decades. She was trained in the discipline at the University of California-San Francisco Medical School, Human Sexuality Program, Sex and Disability Project. (What a mouthful!)

And while it's a fact that chronic illness and disability can occur at any age, I listened in on the call as a baby-boomer whose generation is at the stage in life when health concerns demand more and more of our attention.

What we have not paid so much attention to, though, is the "care and feeding" of our sexuality. It was only in hearing Boyle's encouraging words for the disabled that I saw how mindless we baby-boomers have been about the part of ourselves that so exquisitely unites pleasure and affection.

If those of us who are not disabled could borrow Boyle's prescriptions for those who are, we could have big fun in our mature years.

For even as Boyle speaks about the sexual concerns of the disabled, she offers remedies and encouragement. She tells us that some people with disabilities have a range of physical hurdles to sexual expression: side effects of medications, indwelling catheters, numbness, loss of mobility, changes in muscle tone and sensation, pain or fatigue, bowel and bladder control concerns, erection and ejaculation issues, vaginal dryness.

And some have emotional hurdles, like decreased or absent sex drive, negative body image, depression, grief, or

PART FIVE

Love, Sex, and Disability: The Pleasures of Care

She asked what my name was, and I told her that it was Liv. She said her name was Edna and asked me to pray for her. It was a brief encounter as she helped me open the door to the bank on Broadway. She was a black woman in her 80s who walked with a cane. She asked me why I was using a walker, and when I told her that I had MS, she nodded.

She told me that one of her legs had been amputated and that she was walking with a prosthetic device. She also told me that she had been recently widowed by her Jewish husband and that he had helped her with everything, never uttering a word about her being a burden.

"I guess he knew that disability could happen to him at any time," she said.

I thought about Edna and her husband last week while I was reading *Love, Sex & Disability: The Pleasures of Care* by Sarah Smith Rainey. Rainey takes us into the lives of cohabitating couples where one partner is disabled, and the other is not. She uses words written and spoken by the partners to tell stories about love, sex, and care that most of us are never exposed to.

The disabilities that affect the couples in Rainey's book -- spinal cord injury, cerebral palsy, multiple sclerosis, muscular dystrophy, and vision impairment -- demand intimate care, and require help with basic activities of daily living like bathing, eating, dressing and toileting. Some of the participants in Rainey's study became couples before the onset of the disability; some after. And some met at online dating sites where the disabled partner had to finesse disclosure of their disability after establishing rapport with the nondisabled partner.

erection. In his case, Boyle stressed safety. She advised that he get a good lubricant and avoid using the toy he uses for anal arousal in any other body orifice.

Her messages are clear. When she talks about having sex "whether you have a partner," she is acknowledging that the disabled masturbate just as everyone else does. During the Q&A, a caller spoke about having masturbated for years with sex toys until her disability made it too difficult for her to manipulate them with her hands. Boyle, dauntless, told the caller to ask an occupational therapist to adapt a grip for the sex toys that will make it possible for her to hold them again.

The stories went on and on. I was struck by the honesty of the callers' questions, and by Boyle's speaking about such sensitive matters in a caring, grownup way. I found myself wondering whether having a disability helps people abandon the social masks we're so used to wearing.

For Boyle, sexuality encompasses a great deal more than the physical aspects of sexual expression. She urges us to reject the narrow notion that ejaculation and orgasm are the only "real sex". For many who are disabled, she says, these elements of sex will belong to the past. And there will be a time in the future when they will also lie in the past for older adults who are not disabled.

What belongs to the present for both, though, is the possibility for good communication, cooperation and creativity, ingredients essential for maintaining and enhancing intimate relationships.

And here is where older adults can learn from the experiences of the disabled: "real sex" for us -- both now and in the future – will be whatever turns us on and brings us pleasure.

PART FIVE

I was interested in disabled/nondisabled intimate relationships because if we're going to have intimate romantic relationships as older adults, we are destined to be both caregivers and care receivers I wanted to see what insights Rainey's younger disabled/nondisabled couples (average age 39) could offer us older folks.

Rainey's study covers a vast landscape. She writes about the gender bias inherent in the intimate care narrative. It is assumed that because women are mothers, caregiving is natural for us and that we are expected to take care of our disabled partners. In her study, though, a majority of the nondisabled caregivers were men, and their style of caregiving was more managerial and less subject to burnout than the style of women caregivers. Indeed, the men said that caregiving had made them better men. (I thought about Edna's husband when I read about that.)

Rainey also writes about how TV and movies have made us think of disabled persons as asexual. (The same can be said about how TV and movies depict older adults.) She reviewed historical accounts of the nonconsensual sterilization of the "disabled" to prevent them from having children, and she discussed "erotic segregation" of the disabled as similar to the cultural taboos that were advanced about interracial sex.

The disabled/nondisabled couples in Rainey's study had all received negative messages from family and friends. They were connected to disability support groups, though, and were aware that their relationship was a radical departure from what society views as normative. The same is going to be true for those of us who enter mature relationships with a partner who is already disabled.

Rainey writes about sex for the disabled/nondisabled couples in her study, and here's where mature couples can perhaps learn the most: When one's body is different, sexual activity and intimacy may also be different. The "normal" sexual position – missionary position – may be impossible, for example, for a man with a spinal cord injury. Depending on the disability, genitals may not work as we expect them to, stamina may be impaired, and appearance may deviate greatly from what is culturally endorsed.

The study's couples said that the trust, intimacy, and closeness they feel because of the "caring" they share, however, enhances the sex they have and makes it more pleasurable. The subtitle of Rainey's book says it all: The Pleasures of Care.

One of Rainey's resources, Nel Noddings, writes that when caring works, the couple is locked into a mutually reinforcing connection:

Clearly, the cared-for depends upon the one caring. But the one caring is also oddly dependent upon the cared–for.

So, the take away from the Rainey study for us older adults is this:

Reciprocal caring between loving partners can connect our bodies to each other in an intimate bond that is hotter and more pleasurable than we could ever imagine.

PART SIX

THE DIY BOUDOIR

PART SIX

The Body as Boudoir

The human body likes pleasure. We are born with a cache of chemicals that are released inside our bodies just to make us feel good. Mother Nature likes it that way. Our genes like it, too, when we feel good, and are programmed to replicate these "feel good" codes in the genes of our offspring. "Feeling good" is one of the plusses of being human.

Some of the chemicals in our body are neurotransmitters with names like dopamine and serotonin; some are hormones like oxytocin; and some are the powerful "brain hormones" called *endorphins*. A term whose two parts, *endo and orphin,* are short forms of the words *endogenous and morphine,* the term "endorphin" literally means "internal morphine."

Endorphins are produced by the pituitary gland and hypothalamus, and released into our blood stream during exercise, excitement, pain, consumption of spicy food (now you know why some people put hot sauce on *everything!*), love making and orgasm. Endorphins connect us to pleasure. They give us a feeling of well-being and stimulate euphoric feelings that annihilate stress, depression, and chronic pain.

When we're kids, our parents don't tell us much about enjoying pleasure. (That's probably because they don't want us to overdo the pleasure thing and skip our homework.) We humans, though, begin to get all goofy about pleasure when we're still in our mothers' bellies. Mother Nature sees to that. We have been designed by her, through evolution, to have body components – nerve endings, ductless glands, secretions -- whose sole purpose is to connect us to pleasure. By the time we're born, then, our bodies know all about pleasure and how to create it for ourselves.

PART SIX

It was in a 1987 article in the *Journal of Sonographic Medicine* that researchers first showed the world that human fetuses in the womb – both male and female – know how to masturbate. During one of those basic sonograms pregnant women undergo, a researcher noticed that the fetus on the sonogram screen seemed to be masturbating. A research team soon gathered more data on the phenomenon, published their findings, and a new field of study was born.

Subsequent research observed that fetal masturbation could begin as early as the 15th week of gestation, and that male fetuses used their fingers to stroke their penises, while female fetuses used their fingers to stroke their vulvas and clitorises. It was also observed in the research that the behaviors seen in utero could continue after the baby was born. The language researchers used at the time to characterize the fetal and infant masturbation behaviors was "self-soothing," "self-comforting," and "self-gratifying."

From Mother Nature's point of view, however, engaging in behaviors that bring about pleasure was the point. She had designed our bodies to give us good feelings, and 15 weeks of floating in a watery sac was just about enough time for a fetus to discover how good certain parts of the body could make you feel.

To be sure, the research about fetal and infant masturbation was controversial. In our Judeo-Christian culture, genital stimulation and arousal have been relegated to domains – sex and marriage – that are populated by consenting adults, not babies. So, the idea of an unborn fetus jerking off is a real puzzler: Can an unborn baby commit a sin?

Pro-life/anti-abortion advocates also had a grand time with the research. If a 15-week-old fetus could experience pleasure, then the fetus could also experience pain, their thinking went. It would, therefore, be too late in the pregnancy to perform an abortion. So, for pro-life advocates, the masturbation research served as proof of the claims they'd been making about when life begins.

Until the masturbation research about infants and toddlers was widely circulated, pediatricians and family physicians had been misdiagnosing babies whose parents were presenting a wide range of symptoms. Indeed, the doctors' diagnoses ranged from epilepsy to other "movement" disorders. It was only after researchers saw the similarities – heavy breathing, grunting, sweating, facial flushing, contraction of trunk muscles -- between the orgasm "arc" of infants and toddlers and the arc of "mature" orgasms that they could confirm that the babies had been having orgasms and suggest to doctors that no medical intervention was necessary.

The parents of the masturbating infants and toddlers hadn't known what to do about their babies' unusual behavior and had taken them to the doctor to be examined. Before the masturbation research, the doctors had ordered tests and therapies to address the symptoms the parents described. After dissemination of the research, however, doctors could confidently tell parents not to worry, and that the masturbation behavior was a normal part of child development. Parents could be told to not scold or punish their very young child, or say that their child was doing something wrong, but to wait for an age-appropriate time to introduce the idea of privacy (usually about age 3) and let the child know that the behavior *can* be done in private.

I'm writing all this about fetal and infant masturbation to acknowledge that the capacity to use our bodies for self-pleasuring is built into our DNA. Pleasure is hard-wired into our bodies by Mother Nature. That's why, when I was diagnosed with MS a few years ago, I wanted to go back to the time before I was fully formed and reclaim the part of me that wants to explore all my body's possibilities and boost my enjoyment of life's sensual pleasures. With the MS diagnosis, I began a new chapter of my life, and was determined to put together my own endorphin-releasing program. And even though we don't think of MS and pleasure as BFFs, or intimates, I wanted to uncouple my endorphin-releasing adventures from the persistent reminder that *I'm not the same as I used to be.*

Here are some of the endorphin-releasing activities I found when I looked online:

1. Cardiovascular exercise, e.g., swimming or running
2. Laughter, smiling
3. Having a positive attitude, enthusiasm, cheerfulness
4. Eating spicy food, like chili peppers, horseradish, wasabi
5. Eating dark chocolate
6. Acupuncture
7. Listening to beautiful, calming music
8. Watching a scary movie
9. Riding a roller coaster
10. Meditation
11. Massage
12. Yoga
13. Sex (with or without a partner)
14. Viewing beautiful art
15. Sunshine
16. Crying, expressing emotion
17. Going barefoot, being naked
18. Smelling flowers, cooking food, activities that incorporate smell
19. Gossiping
20. Walking in nature

I'm already doing about 80 percent of the activities on the list, so I'm not that far off the mark. (I'll take a pass, thank you, on the scary movie and roller coaster. Wasabi, yes. Chili peppers, no.)

I'm writing about endorphin-releasing activities today because they're not only good for reducing stress, depression, and chronic pain; they're also good for slowing down the aging process. (For us baby-boomers, that's great news.) One of the websites I visited while I was writing this essay suggested doing several of the endorphin-releasing activities simultaneously to give ourselves a mega-dose of pleasure.

Our body loves for us to pour pleasure into it.

PART SIX

The Bed as Boudoir

Beds are only for sleep or sex. That's what researchers at the National Sleep Foundation – and other sleep experts – tell us about what we should be doing in our beds. Studies show, though, that we are neither sleeping nor having sex there.

A study published by the NSF found that, among married people or couples living together, one-in-four adults skip or avoid sex because they're too tired.

The Better Sleep Council, the trade association that represents the mattress industry, reported that 79 percent of the women it surveyed said they would rather sleep than have sex.

And research data from a variety of sources indicate that about a third of adults in the U.S. are getting less than six hours of sleep at night, shy of the 7 to 9 hours recommended by health professionals. We are a sleep-deprived nation.

Count me among the guilty. I'm a baby-boomer from New York, the 24-hour city where we came of age knowing how-to close-up clubs in the wee small hours, go to after-hour joints, and then head straight to work without breaking a sweat. Sleep deprivation is in my DNA.

For those who do not have that New York *thang*, or who have families and 9 to 5 work commitments, there are countless reasons for sleep loss. Work is more demanding than ever before. Emails and texts extend the work day into the evening hours and weekends. And when we're not working, we have endless to-do lists that lay claim to our diminishing free time.

At night, although we may be in bed, we're not sleeping. Medications, illness, pain, anxiety, insomnia and more keep us from getting the good night's sleep that restores us.

PART SIX

Moreover, our lack of sleep has been linked to obesity, diabetes, and high blood pressure, as well as to negative mood and behavior; decreased productivity; and safety issues in the home, on the job, and on the road. Indeed, the Centers for Disease Control and Prevention has declared insufficient sleep a "public health epidemic."

I'm getting older and I'm ready for a change. I confess that I've not been kind to myself in this area. I'm a night-owl, a writer with an entertainment industry background, and for most of my adult life I've continued the all-niter, coffee-charged, adrenaline-drenched habits I practiced in college.

I should know better. My late father who died a few years ago was a great role model about sleep. He astounded the young residents who examined him in the emergency rooms he frequented during the last year of his life when they learned that, at age 99, he had no chronic illnesses and took no prescription medications.

"What's your secret?" they asked.

"Early to bed and early to rise," he would wink.

What I'm just now understanding, though, is the connection between insufficient sleep and chronic stress. I'm learning that the prolonged elevation of adrenaline and cortisol in the body interrupts normal biological processes – like digestion, excretion, and immune function -- and causes anxiety, depression, insomnia and more.

I am learning that these "stress hormones" also contribute to aging and weight gain.

Indeed, the fat around our bellies is often a symptom that our adrenals are stressed out. It's no wonder we don't want to have sex.

We humans are born with the stress response we need to protect us from danger. We call it the "fight or flight," response, and it's appropriate when we're running from a bear in the woods. The hormones that are released when we're running serve their necessary purpose of heightening our vigilance, and our bodies use them up in the process.

When we're not in true danger, though, and our stress hormones are activated by everyday physical, emotional, or chemical factors, or by such stress producers as inadequate exercise, not eating quality foods – or not getting enough sleep – they are not used up the way they would be when we're running from a bear in the woods. They stay in our bodies as an unconscious, low-level stress condition that keeps us unnecessarily on "alert" all the time.

So, be mindful that that's not a bear lying next to you in bed; that's your sweetie. It's our ever-vigilant, stressed-out bodies that can't tell the difference.

Researchers at the University of California, Berkeley, found that poor sleep made it harder for couples to appreciate their partner. Poor sleep, one researcher said, may make us more selfish as we prioritize our own needs over our partner's.

In other words, the stress conditions most of us now live under make us less available to the feelings we associate with sex and love making. Inadequate sleep makes us more self-protective and less vulnerable to our sweeties.

So, what to do?

A great, easy way to build a bridge between sleep deprivation and intimacy in bed (I didn't say sex, did I?) is to help relieve your partner's stress. Remember that although some of the stress is unconscious, the muscles in the body hold onto it as tension. So, gentle massage, touch, breathing, holding, spooning, kissing, and cuddling are all stress relievers.

Likewise, other senses, can be used to relieve stress: the sound of your voice reading aloud, the sight of a flickering candle, the smell of an aromatic oil, or the taste of a warm beverage.

Don't under estimate what your love and your body can do. Don't under estimate how your empathy and humanity can help rebalance your beloved's well-being.

You can soothe your sweetheart to sleep tonight and give him/her one of the greatest gifts in The Wise Boudoir – sound, restful slumber.

And tomorrow night, the soothing will be for you.

PART SIX

The Bath as Boudoir

As you can see, I'm very interested in how to treat our bodies better – how to love our bodies better. The better we love our own body, I believe, the better we can love our partner's body. That's one of the basic precepts of The Wise Boudoir.

I learned when I was diagnosed with MS that it's an auto-immune disorder in which the myelin sheath that protects the nerve cells in our central nervous system is damaged. MS is not a fatal condition, but everyone with it discovers that certain body functions don't work the way they used to because the brain doesn't work the way it used to.

The symptoms are different for each person and there is no cure for it. Researchers and those who have MS are still trying to understand it and treat it. One way to treat it is to take better care of the body.

I am on the prowl for insights about all this. We can't see our auto-immune response or our central nervous system with our eyes, so we have no idea when they're getting into trouble. We learn that they're in trouble only after the fact.

But no matter our age, or heath status, there are things we can do that our immune systems and nervous systems absolutely love. One is to submerge our bodies in warm water – not to take a bath, but to *have* a bath. Not to wash ourselves, but to be cleansed of our stresses and tensions.

Until the last century when indoor plumbing became widespread, bathing was a social activity. It still is in some cultures. In Japan, for example, Japanese and international tourists flock to *onsen*, a term for "hot spring" in the Japanese language.

PART SIX

As a volcanically active group of islands, Japan has thousands of *onsen* scattered along its length and breadth. *Onsen* water is believed to have healing powers derived from its mineral content. A particular *onsen* might feature several different baths, each with water that has a different mineral composition.

Traditionally used as public bathing places, *onsen* today play a central role in Japan's domestic tourism industry and are favored by families and company groups that want to get away from hectic day-to-day life -- and just relax.

Healing and pleasure are what these baths are for.

That brings us to your bath: Whether yours is a whirlpool, Jacuzzi, hot tub, or an old, glazed cast iron New York City bath tub in a pre-war building (as mine is), submersion in water is perfect for healing and pleasure.

And please be sure to ask your doctor if it's okay for you to soak. Hot baths raise the core temperature in our body and speed our pulse rates. That's not good for everyone. Some MS patients, for example, struggle with heat, and some heart patients struggle with pulse rates.

But if the doc says it will be okay, do yourself a favor.

Fill your tub and drop in for a long, relaxing, moisturizing, detoxifying, and immune- system-boosting soak. A bath can relax your muscles, calm your mind, stimulate your circulation, and clear your lymph system -- all while you're listening to your favorite music.

The health benefits are substantial. Make sure the water is hot enough for you to sweat, though. The deep muscle relaxation is similar to what we experience when we have a massage, and the mental relaxation is like a mini vacation

The increased circulation of the lymph system required for the sweating process will help clear the lymph nodes and create a free-flowing system that removes toxins, bacteria, and viruses from the body. The lymph system is the system responsible for stimulating our immune response and hot baths help increase lymph drainage.

Increased blood circulation will improve all your bodily systems by increasing the rate at which nourishing blood cells get to damaged tissue. In addition, dead cells will be removed from the body more quickly, increasing your ability to stay healthy and energetic.

A hot bath increases both blood and lymph circulation and stimulates your immune system to work more effectively. That's why baths are healing.

Before, during and after your bath, drink water, and allow the bath to cool or add cold water slowly to return your body to its normal temperature and circulation before you get out of the tub.

Use natural oils, such as coconut oil or olive oil, in the water to help moisturize your skin, and a loofa or sea sponge to remove dead skin cells. Do your endocrines a favor, too, and choose natural fragrances, such as essential oils or extracts (one or two drops) to bring aroma to the bath.

Smelling the aroma of essential oils directly affects the limbic part of the brain. The limbic system is highly interconnected with the brain's pleasure center, which plays a role in sexual arousal and the "high" derived from certain recreational drugs.

As I was saying, healing and pleasure.

The next night, turn your sweetie on to the healing and pleasure of a bath that's just like the one you enjoyed. It'll be like yours, but you can raise the stakes for your sweetie and give them a "Bath with Benefits."

Here's how a Bath with Benefits works:
1. Add dim lighting or candles for atmosphere.

2. Place a bath pillow under their neck so they can relax completely.
3. Pour drinks for both of you to enjoy during the bath.
4. Feed them their favorite fruits in bite-sized pieces.
5. Soak a bathing sponge with bath water and run it up and down their body slowly. First, go across their shoulders, then the back, then come around the stomach and move slowly down their legs.
6. When you've covered their entire body, soak the sponge with water again and squeeze t the excess water down their back and chest.
7. After you've sponged their body, use your hands to play "exploration."
8. Enjoy the full sensory experience with your sweetie: the music, the dim lights, the aromas, the fruit, the cool drinks, the relaxation.
9. When the bath ends, unplug the bathtub, and let them rinse off thoroughly in the shower. When they come out, towel dry their body, lay them on the bed and apply a small amount of body cream to their elbows, knees, feet, and anywhere else they might request. Massage anyone?

What's not to like about the Bath as Boudoir?

PART SIX

The Brain as Boudoir

For me, the word *boudoir* has a deeper meaning than the dictionary offers. The *boudoir* I like to write about is our *inner boudoir* – the place we hold inside ourselves for our own healing, comfort, and pleasure.

My claim is that the older we get, the wiser we become about this place and the more motivated we are to take care of it. One way to nourish our inner life is through *play*.

The field of brain science, or neuroscience, has a lot to say about play and the brain.

Neuroscientists have been giving us a heads up that it is important for us to play throughout our lives. Healthy playfulness lowers our stress hormones and keeps our brain processes dynamic, resilient, and adaptive. In other words, play keeps us young.

Over the past couple of decades, *play theory* has become a growing academic discipline and *play scholars* have emerged as gurus on the subject.

Dr. Stuart Brown, often identified as the foremost authority on play behavior, asserts that play is a basic biological drive as integral to our health as sleep or nutrition. Whether it is through physical activity, social interaction, competition, adventure, fantasy or art, our need to play is hardwired into our brains.

Trained in general and internal medicine, psychiatry and clinical research, Dr. Brown first recognized the importance of play by discovering its absence in the backgrounds and life stories of murderers and felony drunk drivers. Scientists now know that when we suppress play at any stage of human development, there are severe consequences.

Founder of the National Institute for Play, Brown believes that when play is woven into the fabric of our social practices, we can transform our personal health, our relationships, the education of our children, and the capacity of our corporations to innovate.

On this latter point, I was awestruck when I saw all the toys (pinball machines, balls, games) in the lounge area of the Google office I visited in Manhattan to tape a *Wise Boudoir* video for You Tube. Google is a 21st century company that understands how much the spirit of playfulness can contribute to creativity and productivity in the workplace. To work at Google is to have fun.

For Brown, *play* is a blissful state of being, and he stresses in his talks that the opposite of play is not work, but *depression*.

He says that play is the gateway to vitality, and is, by its nature, uniquely and intrinsically rewarding. It generates optimism, seeks out novelty, makes perseverance fun, leads to mastery, gives the immune system a boost, fosters empathy, and promotes a sense of belonging and community. Such by-products of play are positive health indicators, he says, and their absence can predict health problems and personal fragility.

And more, Brown asserts that a culture deficient in play places the well-being of its people at risk. The prevalence of depression, stress related diseases, interpersonal violence, addiction, and other health problems can be linked to prolonged deprivation of play.

So, what is play? It is something that's done for its own sake; it's voluntary and it's pleasurable. It is apparently purposeless at the time it's happening. It requires a feeling of being safe – a terrorized or enraged person is not in a position to play. Play gives you freedom from a sense of time and self, Brown says, we're born knowing how to do it, it seems. When a nurturing and loving parent is in a spontaneous encounter with their well-fed and safe infant, the two radiate contagious mutual joy. This hard-wired contagious response is the cornerstone for the child's developing feelings of safety and intimacy.

This is the blissful state of play for both child and parent, Brown says, and accessing this state, as it becomes more complex, is a pre-requisite for the capacity for intimacy throughout life.

Play is good for -- and brings oxygen, refreshment, and nourishment to -- adult-adult relationships, too. Some of its hallmarks are humor, the capacity to share a lighthearted sense of the world's ironies, the enjoyment of mutual storytelling, and the capacity to openly divulge imagination and fantasies. These playful communications and interactions produce a climate for easy connection and intimacy.

Take play out of the mix, and relationships can become a survival and endurance contest. Without play, the repertoire to deal with life's inevitable stresses is narrowed. Even if loyalty, responsibility, duty, and steadfastness remain, without playfulness there will be insufficient vitality left over to keep the adult relationship buoyant and satisfying. This is why it's important for long-term spouses to play with each other.

So, with all that said, how are we doing with play? To be honest, some of us have forgotten *how* to play, or forgotten to ma*ke time* to play.

Brown says that the drive to play does lessen as we mature. The demands of parenthood, for example, are sufficient in our culture, and in most cultures, to require that parents spend a lot of time sustaining a child's life and not much time playing. And since play isn't required for immediate survival; a culture can easily overlook play. Our Judeo- Christian industrial worldview, to be sure, has also lessened the importance of play.

PART SIX

So, there's no cultural norm that would encourage a responsible adult to spend time in fantasy, or to take a half hour off the work day to go out and have fun. Our culture would say that such behavior is irresponsible.

And yet, Brown says, the evidence is solid that if we'd incorporate healthy play into our lives, our performance would be better, our health would be better, and our relationships would be better.

Bernie DeKoven, one of the originators of the New Games movement, has devoted his life to developing games that bring people together -- emotionally -- in the context of play. For those who have forgotten how to play and don't know how to get started again, DeKoven offers the following advice:

You don't have to have rules or goals or a board or even anything to play with except each other. But whatever it is that you're playing, there are two things you have to take seriously: being together, and the sheer fun of it all. No game is more important than the experience of being together ... And no purpose is more uniting and freeing than the purpose of being fun with each other.

When adults play together, they are engaging in exactly the same patterns of behavior that positively shape the brain in children. Close, positive, and emotionally fulfilling relationships heal and create emotional resiliency.

Play provides a safe and joyous context for the development of such relationships. And play is delicious nourishment for your *inner boudoir*.

PART SIX

The Belly as Boudoir

I just called a friend whom I've known for ages to ask her to remind me what she puts in the "special meal" she makes for her husband to "rock his world." She'd told me the story about this meal more than 15 years ago, but I couldn't recall the details. All I could remember was that it was sexy enough for me to remember for 15 years.

I had forgotten that it was just a burger. But it was no ordinary burger; it was a 'rock his world' burger that went like this:

Season freshly ground sirloin with fresh garlic, salt and pepper, and grill burger to taste.

Toast an English muffin in the oven, allowing butter to melt into the nooks and crannies.

Place the burger on the toasted muffin and top it with whipped cream cheese and red caviar.

Serve with a chilled mimosa garnished with fresh fruit.

My friend told me that her husband gave up the ghost when he bit into the pop, ooze and sizzle of the burger and touched the hem of heaven when he sipped the sparkling sweetness of the mimosa right after.

Yeah, food can do all that.

The food superstar I've been able to serve Eric comes from the recipe for a holiday appetizer called Endive Boats. I saw it prepared on my local cable news station, and it goes like this:

Separate and open the leaves of a couple of heads of endive and place them on a platter.

Mix-to-taste a few varieties of bleu cheese and fold heavy cream into the mixture.

Roast a handful of whole walnuts in hot butter in an iron skillet.

PART SIX

Separate the sections of a clementine.

Scoop the cheese mixture onto the endive, place a walnut and slice of clementine on top.

Bite into the crunch of an endive leaf and let the flavors explode in your mouth. Sip a dry, sparkling wine with it, and there you go with the heaven metaphors again. Eric has a nickname for this food, but I won't write it here.

Both treats are high in cholesterol, but sooo good.

Food is a sensual delight that unleashes the hormonal juices I've been writing about in this book. These two recipes are dairy-rich and take us into the "comfort food" world. That's the world of mac and cheese, and other cholesterol-rich foods that make us feel like we want to hug somebody.

It's good for us to know about the foods and natural aphrodisiacs that arouse our bodies and libidos. Knowledge of these foods and seasonings comes to us from both ancient texts and modern science. We can become love-making alchemists in our own kitchens by knowing the secrets of food aphrodisiacs: they increase our blood flow, increase our body heat, and give us hormonal support.

Any food that is good for the heart and circulation is good for sexual health; when blood flows easily, it flows to our genitals, too. And such flow is good for our overall well-being whether we have a partner or not.

So, here we go:

Easy-to-find, blood-flow enhancers include basil, cardamom, ginger, chili peppers, asparagus, watermelon, and pomegranate. Some of these can be used as flavorings in salads, soups, and stews, so don't worry about learning to make a whole dish with them.

Basil, for example, can be chopped and sprinkled over fresh tomato, and cardamom pods can be ground and sprinkled over stir fry. Fresh ginger can also be added to stir fry. If chili peppers are too much for you, try keeping dry cayenne at the ready in your cabinet to sprinkle onto anything you like. I dash a little over my green salads. The blood-flow enhancer, asparagus, can be eaten alone as a side dish, and watermelon and pomegranate can be eaten as a snack or dessert.

Examples of foods that increase our body heat (and you'll notice that some of these appeared earlier as blood-flow-enhancing foods) are cinnamon, nutmeg, coriander, cardamom, chili peppers and ginger. When I wrote the blogpost called the *Bed as Boudoir,* I suggested that you take a warm beverage to your sweetie at bedtime to soothe the tensions of the day. So, sprinkle some ground cinnamon or nutmeg over warm almond milk and watch your partner purr.

Garlic both increases body heat and increases blood flow. It specifically increases blood flow to the male genitals. I just saw an article online explaining that if a man ingests two cloves of garlic a day and washes them down with a glass of pomegranate juice, his level of testosterone and the volume of semen in his ejaculate will increase. The article also said that the results would not happen overnight; he would have to perform the ritual every night for a month to reap any benefits. So, good luck with that one.

The foods that provide hormonal support have natural chemicals that foster sexual desire. The list of such foods includes pine nuts, almonds, pumpkin seeds, oysters, raspberries, avocado, arugula, sea vegetables, anise, honey, sweet potatoes, carrots, and celery. Notably, many are rich in zinc, the chemical that supports healthy prostate glands and the production of testosterone.

Women also need testosterone for good sexual health. Let's all zinc up!

And finally, a word about dark chocolate and red wine. There is serious connoisseurship among those who know chocolates and wines. As I wrote in *The Body as Boudoir*, eating dark chocolate releases in our brain the endorphins that give us the sensation of falling in love. Some folks, like my next-door neighbor, have already found their favorite chocolate and eat a little of it every day.

And here's the news about red wine: *The Journal of Sexual Medicine* published a study about red wine, women, and sex, showing that women who drank 1 to 2 glasses of red wine regularly with dinner had greater sexual desire than women who didn't drink at all, or who drank other alcoholic beverages. The study found that the flavonoids in red wine improved sexual desire by increasing blood flow to key areas of a woman's body.

There's magic and mystery in how our bodies savor food and drink. They arouse juices in us that can urge us toward love and desire or connect us to our deepest satisfactions. When we learn to build mastery in the domain of food and drink, we can treat ourselves and our sweeties to moments of delight can create the kinds of sensations we'll want to revisit again and again.

Our bellies are sensual portals to a private world where we are intimate with ourselves as we may be nowhere else.

PART SIX

The Balm of Touch as Boudoir

My writings for *The Wise Boudoir* have gained a lot from the field of neuroscience and the discoveries researchers make every day about how the human brain works. You can get a Ph.D. today studying many of the activities I've written about play, relaxation, releasing endorphins, and so on. Each of these activities is relevant to the subject of intimacy and relationships for baby-boomers. Each releases into our bodies the hormones that wash over us when we make love.

I found myself struggling the other day when I was talking with someone about how passionate I am about the takeaway message I've gotten from this work: *the more intimacy we have in our lives, the healthier and happier we are.*

Intimacy is good for us in all its forms. Touching. Playing. Gossiping. Kissing.

The person I was speaking with thought I meant only sexual intimacy, so when I mentioned intimacy with oneself, she thought I meant masturbation. I was frustrated and felt like an early adopter of germ theory, arguing in vain with a non-believer that the flu is not possession by an evil spirit, but a virus.

To my rescue came a study in the journal, Emotion, that showed the power of nonsexual touch among players on NBA teams. The researchers concluded the following:

Players who touched their teammates more had higher "Win scores," defined as "a performance measure that accounts for the positive impact a player has on his team's success (rebounds, points, assists, blocks, steals) while also accounting for the amount of the team's possessions that a player uses (turnovers, shot attempts)"

PART SIX

Teams where players touched teammates more also enjoyed significantly superior team performance than those where players touch teammates less.

And here's a list of the kind of "touching" the researchers observed in their study. High fives, chest bumps, leaping shoulder bumps, chest punches, head slaps, head grabs, low fives, high tens, full hugs, half hugs, and team huddles.

Amazing, huh? Each of these nano-second touch encounters had the power to release positive "juice" in a player's body. On average, a player touched other teammates a little less than two seconds during the game, or about one tenth of a second for every minute played. Just imagine what touching someone for an extended time can do. It's why sex, dancing, massage, and other high-contact engagements make us feel so good. We want to connect with one another.

Researchers are learning that touch is truly fundamental to human communication, bonding, and health. It signals safety and trust; it soothes. Basic warm touch calms stress. It activates the body's vagus nerve, which is intimately involved with our compassionate response. And a simple touch can trigger release of oxytocin, aka "the love hormone."

But some Western countries, like the U.S., are "touch deprived." If you go to various other countries, people spend a lot of time in direct physical contact with one another -- much more than we do in the U.S. One study I read observed the conversations of friends in different parts of the world as they sat in a café together. In England, the two friends never touched, and in the U.S., the friends touched each other twice. In France, the pair touched 110 times, and in Puerto Rico 180 times.

You were just an infant when an adult asked your mother or caregiver, "Can I hold the baby?" Imagine the pleasure you gave to the person who wanted to have the wonderful feeling of

PART SIX

holding you. Imagine that holding your tiny frame soothed them, softened their stress, and engaged their care and compassion.

That was you.

When I spoke with Eric on the phone earlier, he told me that he felt a little overwhelmed today by all he has to do to get ready for his solo art exhibit that opens this week and asked me what I do when I feel overwhelmed.

"That's why I have you," I said.

I saw an article the other day saying that we're all overwhelmed these days. With TV news, mobile devices and our being connected to everything, we're exposed to more incoming energy in one day than a person in the 17th century would have been exposed to in a lifetime. Of course, we're overwhelmed.

"But I can quiet all of that with you," I told Eric. "It's touching and holding that soothes, softens, and keeps me sane."

PART SEVEN

INTIMACY WITH OURSELVES

PART SEVEN

Exhibit Yourself Beautifully to Yourself

It all started with an invitation from my friend, Lana, to attend a book launch party at the Strand Bookstore here in Manhattan. Lana is one of the subjects in *Advanced Style: Older and Wiser* by Ari Seth Cohen, a book that features photographs of "senior street style" from cities around the world and short essays by the subjects – including my friend – about their lifestyle secrets.

I went to the event knowing that I would be surrounded that evening by mature women to whom *style* is a way of life and for whom life is still a dazzling adventure. I knew that their audacity to dress with such flair would inspire me to write something about the evening, and to think about the art of dressing for women over 50.

After logging in to Amazon to read a description of the book, I found another one about style called *The Lost Art of Dress: The Women Who Once Made America Stylish* by Linda Przybyszewski. The book narrates the history of fashion in the U.S. in the first half of the 20th century and tells the fashion stories played out by the mothers and grandmothers of us baby- boomers. Sheath dresses, girdles, hats, brooches, gloves, matching pumps. Remember these?

It seems that the women who called the shots back then – whom the author calls "Dress Doctors" – were mostly connected to the now-defunct home economics departments -- at colleges, high schools, and junior high schools -- where learning how to dress and how to sew were part of a young girl's education.

Girlhood, since the 19th century, had been a time when a young girl prepared for the roles she would assume as wife, mother, and the moral/spiritual center of her family. Becoming an adult was a big deal for her. Good character was what she was supposed to develop, and the ideals of duty, honor, modesty, and integrity were superior to "looking cute." Home economics departments were places where a girl's way of dressing and presenting herself were matched to the social values she was learning.

These departments were also places that distinguished between the clothes a young woman *should* wear and the clothes a mature woman *could* wear. Sophisticated styles were reserved for older women because such styles typically draped and clung to the body. They revealed the subtle eroticism of women who were old enough to have filled out their body's curves, and responsible enough to handle money, feed the children, run the household -- and have sex. Sophisticated styles were not for young, unmarried women.

Przybyszewski tells us that the Dress Doctors liked knowing that the Paris fashion houses back then were targeting woman over thirty as their customers, asserting that only with maturity could a woman wear clothes "with an air of smartness and chic." The author says that the head of salons at Nina Ricci maintained, as late as 1964, that it was nearly impossible for a young model to show off a sophisticated ensemble to advantage; only an older woman would know how to *move* in it, the salon director often said.

The Dress Doctors wrote the style textbooks, and, with magazine editors, designers, retailers, and fashion industry doyennes, set the standards for how a woman should dress until the baby-boomer generation turned the fashion world upside down. Starting in the 1960s, the baby-boomer "Youthquake" introduced the jeans and T-shirt look and discarded the styles their elders had worn.

PART SEVEN

By then, a significant shift had taken place in society's attitudes toward both age and fashion. Przybyszewski argues that as the teenage figure became the new cultural ideal, and growing up no longer seemed a worthwhile goal, the styles meant for womanly figures were largely forgotten. Yes, baby-boomer girls did pass into adulthood, but they did so, without the Dress Doctors' healthier attitudes toward mature women, Przybyszewski says, and without their insights on how to flatter the mature woman's body.

Home economics programs had been eliminated from schools by the mid-1970s on the grounds that they were passé and encouraged gender stereotypes. Manufacturers of women's clothes had abandoned what they called "Sophisticated Styling" in favor of "Youthful Styling." Moreover, Sophisticated Styling didn't matter in an era when "women shop in misses departments along with their daughters *and* granddaughters," one noted Dress Doctor observed.

Youthful styling for all ages soon became casual dressing for all ages. And casual dressing may have led to *casualness* in other areas of living, many say. When we stop making an effort to dress for ourselves while we're at home alone, it easily follows, we will soon forget how to exhibit ourselves beautifully to ourselves.

Thank heaven for the subjects in *Advanced Style* who have the heart to present themselves beautifully. One of the women on the program at the Strand event was more than ninety years old and pleaded with members of the audience to look into our mirrors to see our beauty. She urged us to appreciate our eyes, nose, ears, and to thank all our body parts for serving us so well.

I thought about the self-appreciation the speaker invited us to indulge as I leafed through the pages of *Advanced Style,* and saw one example after another of beautiful, mature women.

PART SEVEN

Beauty elevates, I thought. It encourages us to do beautiful things. It encourages us to have respect for ourselves, those we love, and those with whom we come into contact every day.

I'm reminded now of an old boyfriend from years ago who commented on the frumpy clothes I was then wearing around the house. "Why do women want to 'hag' us out?" he asked one day. I never forgot that. I had to honestly ask myself whether I wanted to be a 'downer' or a 'lifter-upper' in my lover's life. I'm also thinking now of the story one of my girlfriends told me about visiting her elderly aunt in the hospital. She had noticed that her aunt's equally elderly roommate was wearing a beautiful rose-colored negligee as she lay in her hospital bed waiting for her husband's visit. (She certainly wasn't trying to 'hag' him out!)

Beauty lifts the spirit and inspires optimism. It's hard to feel down when you look beautiful. And it's also hard for those around you to feel down. The human soul and eye crave beauty, so dressing beautifully is a gift to all.

The rich vocabulary of dress for mature women is long gone, but the grace and wisdom we have gained with time and experience give us an exquisite canvas on which to sketch new images of beauty. Our mature faces express strength and thoughtfulness as well as the marks of worries. The muscles in our mature bodies hold the memory of both triumph and tragedy. Our mature hearts beat with the desire to behold the beautiful in ourselves.

The Dress Doctors had it right. One explained that the difference between mere clothing and well-designed clothing "is not one of the quantities, or outlay or even of degree, but a subtle and important quality *that lifts them from the realm of mere physical necessity into one where the spirit also is refreshed.* Another said that dress is more than practicality: *"It is the means of expressing your love of beauty and of life."*

PART SEVEN

The women whose photographs populate Advanced Style have much to teach us about beauty and mature style. We can start with the lessons we learn from them and build from there. We can learn to practice the art of being beautiful even when we're at home alone. We can learn to treat ourselves with the same affection and attention we'd offer a lover. We can learn to create luxurious rituals for ourselves to elevate our mood and our wellbeing. We can learn to honor ourselves by taking pleasure in the simple joys of life.

And if we're really good students, we can again learn the finesse and care of exhibiting ourselves beautifully to ourselves.

PART SEVEN

I Want to be Like Her When I'm Her Age

On Thanksgiving Day, I went to my church's community room for dinner and sat at a table with a woman I'd never seen before. She was the cousin of someone I used to sing with in the choir, and I'd chosen a seat next to her because she looked so friendly. She told me that she was 92 years old, and I could barely believe it. She wore a short, white Afro, a skirt and sweater set, leather boots, and looked twenty years younger than she was.

  She was engaging, spirited and ready to have a good time. I watched her laugh and chat with the folks who had prepared the annual feast, and smiled as she enjoyed a fruity treat from the dessert table before the dinner was served. I watched her beam with delight when a new platter was put on the appetizer table that was already flush with finger foods and goodies.

  "Wanna try some of the shrimp they just put out?" she twinkled. "I think they're hot." She dashed over to the appetizers and walked back to our table keeping time with the oldies that were playing on the PA speakers. She offered me the piping hot shrimp from a small paper plate, and we giggled as we downed the tasty appetizer, nodding with approval about how well seasoned the shrimp were.

  We talked a little about her life, about how she had learned to drink her coffee black at the NYU data entry job from which she had long ago retired, and about her late husband whose walker she still has in her apartment in case the day comes when she'll need to use it.

  "You should get a husband," she said to me.

PART SEVEN

I changed the subject quickly and told her that Eric was already on his way. He had been serving Thanksgiving Dinner at his own church, I told her.

Marriage seemed to be one of her favorite topics, so she continued to survey the others at the table. She asked the older man who was eating his second helping of salad about his wife, and he told her he had never been married. He said that he had always lived alone, but sometimes yearned for a home-cooked meal.

"Nobody cooks anymore," she said. "I buy the ready-made dinners they have at the supermarket and call it a day."

But when her cousin's husband sat down at the table, she was thrilled to tell the lifelong bachelor that her cousins had been married for 60 years.

"Sixty years," she stressed. "Married 60 years."

I've known her cousins, Katy, and Nat, for that long, it seems. I was a little kid when they married in the 1950s and saw them serve as church officers alongside both my late mother and late father. They were married by the church's founding pastor and have remained foundational to our shrinking church community. A 60-year marriage anywhere is rare.

Eric arrived while we were sharing church memories, and we all introduced ourselves. I wanted him to know that the woman who was having such a good time at our table was 92 years old, so I called her over to our seats.

"I want to be like her when I'm 92," I told him, holding her hand and his. "I can see why," he said.

We dove into our dinner plates and filled ourselves with as much turkey and fixings as our bellies would allow. Over dessert, we began talking about our 92-year-old friend again, and, this time, Eric beckoned her over.

PART SEVEN

"We could get rich if we could put that energy you have into a bottle. What is it?" he asked her.

"Just be happy. That's all," she said. "Be happy."

Later, as the festivities drew to a close, and as the dining tables were cleared away, people began dancing to the music that blared from the speakers.

"Let's dance," said the 92-year-old woman to Eric.

I want to be like that when I'm her age. I want to be enthusiastic, spontaneous, youthful, friendly, sensual, curious -- and happy.

Her way of being is a real inspiration.

PART SEVEN

Born to Be Intimate

We are born this way. Intimacy is in our DNA.

The other day, I saw a woman with one of those convertible baby carriages sitting at a table across the aisle from me in my favorite coffee shop. When I asked her how old the baby was and heard her say, "Four," I assumed she had said, "Four months."

"So, he's a new baby," I said.

"No," she said, "he's four years old and just likes to sit like that."

Indeed, when I looked deeper into the carriage, I saw the toddler sleeping upright in the position we associate with a fetus in the womb. His back was curled against the support of the carriage, his chin was tucked his head against his chest, and his arms and legs were dangling in front of his belly. The canopy that covered the carriage kept it dark inside.

"We all remember that feeling somehow, don't we?" I said. "Yes, we do," she said.

I was so struck by what I had seen that, when I got home, I went to Google to read more about the world inside the womb and the instinct to connect with our mothers that's with us from birth. I found several websites that took me there.

It is common knowledge that in the womb, all our needs are met. We are fed with nutrients from the placenta, kept warm by heat from our mother's body, and comforted by cushioning from the amniotic fluid that surrounds us. That fluid also keeps us buoyant, so we are able to move freely in a dark, secure, floating world where we hear the muffled sound of our mother's voice and the constant, reassuring thump of her heartbeat.

PART SEVEN

After we are born, our instincts kick in. As we adjust to a world full of unfamiliar sounds and sensations, we may calmly take it all in, or we may make our presence felt the only way we know how and cry out loud with all our might. It's a shock to move from our secure, dark floating world into reality.

We can be soothed by the familiar, though. The sound of our mother's voice and skin-to- skin contact with her warm body allow us to feel the comfort of closeness. When we are placed on her chest, we hear her familiar heart rhythm and absorb her heat. As newborns, we aren't able to regulate our own body temperature and can soon become chilled. So, keeping us warm also soothes us. Dimming the lights in the room we're in helps our eyes to adjust.

We are born with several powerful reflexes and are genetically programmed to bond with our mothers through touch and smell. We grasp her thumb if she places it in our palm and turn our head towards her if she brushes our cheek. These reflexes are precursors to the breastfeeding experience. And, as we take in our mother's scent, grasp for her nipples, move towards her breasts, and prepare to feed, we are fulfilling the destiny of all who are born to be intimate.

We are also genetically programmed to feel good when certain chemicals, or hormones, are at high levels in our bodies. The hormone oxytocin, which is released throughout a pregnancy and in greater amounts during labor and breastfeeding, is widely known as the *bonding* hormone. Its role in the birthing process is to help mother and baby survive the strains of childbirth. But it does much more than that.

Oxytocin sets the stage for our experience of intimacy in later life by engaging the "reward centers" that light up when we fall in love. Also released during orgasm, oxytocin has been called the *love* hormone because it makes us feel good about the person with whom we shared the orgasm.

In our bodies, oxytocin partners with other feel-good brain chemicals such as endorphins, dopamine, and serotonin to become important pillars of our positive physical wellbeing. And here's where my experience of the toddler took me: His peaceful nap in the dark carriage with his intimate at his side reminded me that there was a time when I was being washed in these hormones and being prepared for love.

We all start out this way. A mother's body floods with oxytocin the moment a baby decides to be born. That means we are all hardwired for intimacy and love. It's a great way to come into the world, isn't it?

PART SEVEN

What Makes an Older Woman Sexy?

Yesterday, I got a call from a friend inviting me to join a small group of women at her home this evening to see a demonstration of products that promise to diminish the lines around my eyes and reduce the folds growing under my chin. I declined her invitation, even though the young Spanish-speaking guy who just delivered my morning coffee and muffin greeted me as "señora."

Today, First Lady Michelle Obama turned 50, and in an interview with *People Magazine* said that she doesn't plan to do anything to her face any time soon. Good for you, Michelle. When asked about Botox injections or a facelift, she said, "Right now, I don't imagine that I would go that route, but I've also learned to never say 'never'."

"Women should have the freedom to do whatever they need to do to feel good about themselves," she added.

Mrs. Obama is a late baby-boomer who was born in 1964, the last year of the post-World War Two phenomenon that gave our generation its name. By the millions, baby-boomers are having aesthetic cosmetic surgery as well as less-invasive procedures like Botox injections.

According to the most recent report from the American Society of Plastic Surgeons (ASPS), cosmetic surgery is an $11 billion business, and an estimated 14.6 million procedures were performed in the U.S. in 2012. The Society identified the top five procedures in 2012 for all age groups as breast augmentation, nose reshaping, eyelid surgery, liposuction, and facelift.

The garden-variety facelift has been decreasing among older women for more than a decade, however, because of the popularity of such minimally invasive injectable wrinkle fillers as Botox. Since 2000, these treatments have increased nearly sevenfold, and the ASPS estimates that some 3.3 million women over the age of 55 had such injections in 2012.

And while I agree with Michelle Obama that a woman should be free do whatever she needs to do to feel good about herself, I was inspired by blogger, Ellary Eddy, Editor/Publisher of Realize Magazine.com, who dives deeper into quality-of-life issues for older women, and asks: W*hat is it that makes an older woman sexy?*

Below, I've excerpted her post from the November 12, 2013, issue of *The Huffington Post* where she captures qualities, I'd like to cultivate for *The Wise Boudoir*. Enjoy.

First of all, it's how a woman inhabits her body. No matter the size or shape -- is it her temple? Does she treasure it? Is she proud of it? Does she own it? A woman who owns her body, is just damn sexy. Every shape has its attendant curves and delights; a woman who knows how to display them just plain rocks. And let's not forget the structural elements, the bones, many of which, as the flesh shifts, gain more presence, more sculptural gravitas. Consider shoulders, consider hips, consider the back...

Add to that the way a woman moves her body, not simply in bed, but everywhere she goes. It's like a signature, maybe funny and abrupt, maybe languorous, and full of grace. It's something every woman should contemplate -- how much is conveyed by the way she moves as well as by the sound of her voice. A cultivated female voice is something which only grows more alluring with age. Don't forget how much sex occurs in the dark. A resonant voice, a voice modulated for allure, a 'come hither' voice, can unbutton any psyche. A woman who has control over the tone, the inflection, and the colors, can float you on the oscillations, on the waves of her voice.

But a voice is rudderless without a mind. What in fact is the sexiest part of anyone? The mind -- for that is what creates the context, spins the tale. Knowing when to stroke, when to resist, when to yield, when to quicken, when to slow... when to submit, when to dominate, when to make a sudden volte-face... And let's banish any doubt -- an older mind, or shall we say a sophisticated mind, filled with experience and stories and years of observation, can knock a younger one out of the ring.

Then there are the eyes. The power that emanates can cause spontaneous combustion. And of course, the mouth. It can hunt with agility at any age, and again, years of experience make it a formidable adversary to any prey that it targets.

Of course, the historic 'refuge' of the older woman is her style. Unquestionably some of the most wonderfully dressed females on the planet now are over 50. The reason is that they understand what works for them, what flatters them... so their style is unique, often above and beyond trends. And that is just plain sexy. Self-awareness is sexy.

But my favorite element is the laugh (which is of course linked to the voice). The way a woman laughs, how easily and how often, how hard she laughs, how lilting her laugh. Does she giggle, chuckle, chortle, guffaw; does she snort :)? To laugh is to open.

And so let us laugh, Darlings, because the paramount quality that makes a woman sexy is her outlook on life. If she laughs without measure, you know she derives great joy from life, has the ability to transcend pain and grief and still find pleasure in the mere fact of her existence.

And is this not the most appealing element of any human -- their ability to feel and express joy? To me, this is our single most captivating virtue and one which, in my mind at least, is infinitely sexy.

PART SEVEN

My Wise Boudoir Birthday

Last week, I turned 65 and Eric and I celebrated with two kinds of cake and a Prosecco toast. (He claims that I drank the whole bottle by myself, but who cares? It was my birthday!) The day before, I treated myself to a deep massage at the spa, and the day after, a girlfriend took me to the theatre to see an ensemble of amazing actors – led by the legendary Cicely Tyson -- in *A Trip to Bountiful*.

During the whole week, I thought about how grateful I am for the intimacy I have in my life and how much it nourishes me. The intimacy of place, family, tribe, community, friendship, memory, caring, compassion, and connection energize me and sustain my feeling of well-being. The play, with Tyson at the helm, stirred all these for me.

A Trip to Bountiful, by Horton Foote, is the story of Carrie Watts, a woman in her 80s who yearns to visit the place where she grew up – the place she calls 'home' -- one last time. Against the judgment of her adult son and daughter-in-law, she travels alone to the long-abandoned town of Bountiful, Texas to "feel the soil" in her fingers again.

Watts' yearning reminded me of my late father's longing in his mid-90's to travel back to Florence, South Carolina, my parents' home town, and to visit Wilson High School where, in the 1920s, he had been the quarterback on the football team and trombonist in the school's marching band. He died in 2009 at the age of 99, and never made it back.

Founded originally as an elementary school by the Freedman's Bureau for formerly enslaved black people after the Civil War, the school was eventually named for Joshua E. Wilson, the great-grandfather of a friend of mine. Wilson had been elected to Congress during Reconstruction but was prevented from holding office by wily Southern Democrats. A loyal Lincoln Republican, Wilson was confirmed by the U.S. Senate, instead, to serve as Florence County's Postmaster for four consecutive terms, from 1876 to 1899. Florence, South Carolina is my Bountiful and home to both sides of my family. Storied and mythic, it is my connection to tribe.

The play also enveloped me in the intimacy of community. Carrie Watts sings to herself all day long, and as portrayed by Cicely Tyson, who won a Tony for the role, sings hymns and spirituals from the black church. At the Saturday matinee I attended, the audience joined her in several songs that everyone seemed to know. She became the conductor and we, the congregation. Spontaneously familiar, we were intimates in our music heritage:

Softly and tenderly, Jesus is calling, Calling for you and for me;
See, on the portals he's waiting and watching, Watching for you and for me.
Come home, come home, Ye who are weary, come home!
Earnestly, tenderly, Jesus is calling, Calling, oh sinner, come home!

And then there was the intimacy of friendship after the play when my friend and I strolled through Times Square looking for a place to grab a bite to eat. This was the first time she had walked with me while I was using a cane, so I appreciated her caring and patience. One of my MS symptoms is an unsteady gait, so she lent support to me as we moved through the crowded streets. Over dinner, we talked about our health, our deceased parents, our creative projects, our triumphs, and our frustrations. We connected.

Other friends called during the week with birthday wishes, and my favorite calls were from those who have been my school mates and know exactly how old I am. They, too, have turned or

PART SEVEN

will be turning 65 this year. And theirs was a tone of "Well, kiddo, this is it. How're you making out?"

What remains unspoken in our exchange is our compassionate witness to each other's lives. I don't notice or comment on their sags, squints, or slumps. And they don't comment on mine.

Maybe the reason I now like to spend time with one of my teachers from high school (she'll be treating me to a birthday dinner next week) is that, with her, I'll always be the bright little freshman who came into her typing class wanting to know why the keyboard had no letters on it. Perspective is everything. Little did I know when I met her that she had just graduated from college, and mine was the first class she had ever stood in front of!

If Socrates is known for having said, "Know thyself," the takeaway from my 65th birthday celebration is "Nourish thyself." Nourish thyself with loving friends, art, family, spirituality, community, and a deep connection to life.

I believe that's what really happening in The Wise Boudoir.

PART SEVEN

With Whom are You Intimate?

I called some intimates last weekend and discovered that I was calling parts of myself, too. I called my best friend from high school, and we did some catching up. She recently secured tenure as a full professor at the university that hired her a few years ago, and just donated black theatre (Negro Ensemble Company) ephemera to the Smithsonian. She's now in the market for a used car, and we talked a little about *Car Facts* dot com and the fact that we can learn about nearly anything we want on the internet. We giggled about the quirks of life the same way we did in high school. She reminds me that I've always had a wicked sense of humor.

    I called my oldest living relative who had asked me to call her more often when we spoke earlier this month. I'd gone to her lavish 80th birthday celebration a decade ago and had a great time meeting some of the people who love her. Real estate and New York City are her passions. so, I told her the latest news about luxury condos in Manhattan. Now having Parkinson's and increasing dementia, she's thinking about an assisted living facility. She reminds me that a simple phone call from me can mean a lot to an intimate.

    I called a dear friend who is also a former business associate. He's a Harvard MBA guy whose focus today is Obamacare and health insurance. He checks in with me frequently to see how I'm doing in the MS world, and I check in to see how he's doing with his new business. We share politics and values and talk a lot about history and world events. I told him about the new releases I found in the local book store I visit each week when I

PART SEVEN

go grocery shopping and emailed one of the new titles to him after we spoke. He reminds me that I love the world of ideas.

I called my teacher from high school who is also a member of my church and leads the mentorship program that I've participated in there. She called me earlier in the week to see how I was doing, and I was returning her call. We spoke about the young people in the mentorship program and about one of the group's founders who passed away this year. We brainstormed a little about what the program's next steps might be and agreed to get together for dinner. She reminds me how important my connection to community still is.

I called my oldest friend from the Harlem neighborhood where I grew up. I've known him since I was 8 years old, and he's retired now. We went to high school together and were shaped by the same social and political tides that influenced our community in the 1950s and 1960s. He is the older brother I never had, and his wisdom has always meant a lot to me. He's a jazz lover and I'd heard some music on the radio that I wanted to tell him about. His taste and mine are cut from the same post-war cloth. He reminds me of the old days and of how square I really am.

I called a close friend of 30 years with whom I have shared journeys through art and culture, spirituality, entrepreneurship, relationships with men, the world of work, personal growth and more. She just received her MFA in playwriting and is ready for what will be next in her life. I saw a Hmong author on cable TV last week whose book speaks to the people in my friend's thesis play, and I wanted to tell her about it. We listen to one another with great care, and I am deeply moved whenever I speak with her. She reminds me that friendship is a nonjudgmental place where I can stretch and grow.

And I called my sweetheart, Eric, who reminds me that I'm a woman whose voice can charm, seduce, cajole, admonish, delight, reassure, correct, invite and more. It is through intimacy with him that I am reminded of the womanly part of me who lives in my flesh like a secret code. She's a mystery to me in many ways, but I know she's there. Eric reminds me that I may never know this part of me because she lives only in the heart of her special other.

    These are intimacies that make me who I am today. I'm beginning to see that these parts of me can only exist if there is someone with whom I can share myself.

    So, I thank these intimates for being in my life.

PART SEVEN

Self-Care? Care!

I'm a believer now. Self-care is essential. It's more tedious than self-gratification, to be sure, and requires us to be closer to ourselves than we may be used to. It requires an intimacy with our own well-being that will call us back to ourselves when we drift too far away.

Yesterday, I went to see my physical therapist, and he tested my performance on several tasks whose outcomes he periodically reports to my insurer. During the session, I noticed that my performance was not as strong as it had been the last time, he tested me. I knew that lately I hadn't been exercising as regularly as I should as an MS patient, and that my functionality was already paying the price. I also knew that it takes time for the body to adjust to a more aggressive exercise regimen, and that I had a lot of work ahead if I wanted to do better on the test next time.

But there was someone else in the picture that I had not been paying attention to. That "someone else" is the insurer. The insurer is monitoring the effectiveness of my exercise program through the reports my physical therapist sends, and the insurer wants to be sure that the extended therapy it covers is helping me to maintain my functionality.

"If you let yourself go," the insurer can say, "we'll let you go, too."

And then, I got another wake-up call when I went to see my regular doctor and asked him why he wants me to have blood tests so often. I was crabby about having my arm poked every other month and felt that the frequent blood tests might not be necessary because I keep getting the same results.

PART SEVEN

The doctor explained that the high blood pressure meds I take every day are putting wear- and-tear on my body as my liver and kidneys process their absorption. He also told me that he wants to see my lab workup more often than the twice-a-year check-ins Medicare recommends. He wants to make sure that my internal organs are okay.

"Oh," I said.

Self-care is no joke. Wikipedia defines it as "any necessary human regulatory function which is under individual control, deliberate and self-initiated." In other words, self-care is the practice of taking care of oneself.

How we're taking care of ourselves as adults over 50 is a topic that comes up nearly every time I talk with a friend. It's a big deal for us now. Nowadays, we listen to each other carefully to see whether there are insights about diet, exercise, sleep, and meds that might be useful to us. We all seem to be struggling to find the best regimen. We're all doing some version of trial-and-error.

The Wikipedia article on self-care also, surprisingly, directed me to the late 20th century French philosopher, Michel Foucault, and his writings on how taking care of oneself was also a big deal for the ancient Greeks and Romans. For them, it wasn't the mani-pedi kind of self-care we think of today, but an ethical imperative that was part of the *art of living*.

I wanted to know more about what the ancients had to say about self-care, so I picked up Foucault's posthumous book, *The Care of the Self*, the third volume of his larger work, *The History of Sexuality*. In it, Foucault tells us that the ancients considered a well-cared-for body to be essential for sexual pleasure (which the Greeks called *aphrodisia*), as well as for excellence in every other aspect of human life. He writes about how caring for the self, in the ethics of the ancients, went beyond caring for one's body, and included caring for one's soul.

When Foucault discusses Plato's *Apology,* for example, he says that it was as a master of the *care of the self* that Socrates addressed the judges at his trial and admonished them to be concerned not with their riches or their honors, but with their souls. Later, Foucault quotes the philosopher, Epictetus, who writes that care of the self is a privilege, a gift, a duty, and an obligation in which we learn to see ourselves as the "object of all our diligence."

The term the Greeks used to describe the obligation to take care of oneself, *epimeleia,* encompasses a lot: It is *epimeleia* that describes the activities of the master of a household, the tasks of the ruler who looks after his subjects, the care that must be given to a sick or wounded patient, as well as the honors that must be paid to the gods or to the dead.

With regard to oneself, Foucault says, *epimeleia* implies a labor that takes time. And time is one of the big problems, says Foucault, in determining the portion of one's day or of one's life that should be devoted to caring for oneself.

Here, I'm reminded of my late father whom I always thought would have made a great Stoic. He was diligent about self-care, and firm, for example, about having regular meal times and a regular bedtime. My feelings were hurt, as a kid *and* as an adult, when our time together had to come to an end because of his self-care commitments. At such times, it seemed that our father-daughter relationship was less important to him than his lunch, and I resented it. When he died at the age of 99, his health was excellent for a man his age; he took no prescription meds at all. I get it now: Making time to care for yourself can sometimes cause conflict with others, even as it preserves the deeper promise you have to yourself.

PART SEVEN

To be sure, the ancient Greeks lived in a different world than we do. By our lights, they were pagans, slaveholders, homophobes, and patriarchal misogynists whose superstitions about sex would make us laugh. They had some enduring ideas, though, about care of the body and the soul that we can practice as mature adults (as my father did) today.

I've taken these thoughts from the book's second section, *The Cultivation of the Self:*

There is the care of the body to consider, health regimens, physical exercises without overexertion, the carefully measured satisfaction of needs. There are the meditations, the readings, the notes one takes on books or on conversations one has heard, notes that one reads again later, the recollection of truths that one knows already, but that need to be more fully adapted to one's own life.

One can set aside a few moments, in the evening or in the morning, for introspection, for examining what needs to be done, for memorizing certain useful principles, for reflecting on the day that has gone by. One may also, from time to time, interrupt one's ordinary activities and go into one of those "retreats" that enable one to commune with oneself, to recollect one's bygone days, to place the whole of one's past life before one's eyes, to get to know oneself, through reading, and, by contemplating a life reduced to its essentials.

It is possible, too, at the end of one's career, to unburden oneself of certain activities, and, taking advantage of one's declining years when desires are calmed, to give oneself up entirely to the possession of oneself.

As I dove deeper into all of this, I learned that many ancient philosophers acknowledged the influence of Egyptian wisdom traditions on Greek thought. Indeed, the famous aphorism attributed to Socrates, "Know Thyself", is inscribed on one of the walls at the Temple of Luxor (Thebes) in Egypt. The Temple of Luxor dates to 1400 BCE, so people have been thinking about self-care a long time!

PART SEVEN

In his public lectures in the 1980s, Foucault talks about how self-care lost its importance in the West. He doesn't discuss the idea in the book, but in other venues suggests that four developments pulled us away from the culture of self-care that had been central to the ancients.

He calls the first development the "ethical paradox of Christianity" in which renouncing oneself became a way of glorifying God. The second was the spread of education and the incorporation of many of the ancient self-care practices into basic schooling. The third was the development of science in which human knowledge gradually replaced superstition as the basis for self-care. (In the Greco-Roman world, for example, sex was thought by some to be "dangerous" for one's health.) And the fourth was the development of what Foucault calls the "hidden self". Here, he refers to Freud and other thinkers who probed the "invisible" domains of being human.

I hear rumblings that people are being pulled toward self-care in a new way today. It is precious to our well-being no matter how old we are. Like others, I'm struggling to carve out time each day to make it an important part of my life. I'm challenged, though, to have an intimacy with my own well-being that lifts self-care as a personal pleasure and not just another chore.

Seneca, one of the Roman philosophers in Foucault's book, talks about the pleasure of self-care in the "letters" he wrote after retiring from his post in the Emperor Nero's court. Seneca was then an older adult, and, for him, self-care was more than the obligation to be responsible for oneself: It was an opportunity to take pleasure in oneself.

Through self-care, Seneca said, we "gain access" to ourselves, learn to delight in ourselves, and become objects of our own pleasure. (Who wouldn't want to set aside time every day for that?) Unlike other pleasures, says Seneca, the pleasure of self-care is not caused by anything independent of ourselves, but arises out of ourselves and within us. For older adults, our feelings of pleasure connect us to our aliveness and our aliveness, in turn, connects us to feelings of pleasure. I like pleasure, and I like knowing that the pleasure of self-care lies within me. And more, I like knowing that my desire to feel this pleasure will be there to call me back to myself if I drift too far away.

PART SEVEN

Intimacy and Vulnerability

I saw a panel of relationship "experts" on TV a few years ago, and the panelist who left the greatest impression on me said that true intimacy required *vulnerability*. I've been thinking about what he said for a long time and asking myself in what ways I might be expressing vulnerability in my relationships.

The question of vulnerability came up for me last week when I was listening to a woman my age tell the women who had gathered for a holiday dinner about an accident that had happened in her kitchen. As she tried to pour a pot of boiling water into a large glass pitcher, the glass broke, and boiling water scorched her legs. The accident left her with very serious burns on her upper thighs and a night with burn specialists in the hospital.

By the time she came to the holiday gathering, her burns had been carefully bandaged, and the healing had begun. She is a dance instructor and found herself pondering deeper meanings of the accident.

"The burns were only a half-inch from my vulva," she told us.

I felt myself quiver. A half-inch from this tender part of a woman's body is a close call, indeed. The vulva is extremely sensitive to pleasure and pain because of the huge number of nerve endings in the organ. Nerve endings in the human body are responsible for us feeling any external changes and there are about 8000 nerve endings in the vulva. Injuries to the vulva are rare, however, because the structure itself offers natural protection.

The vulva is a metaphor for the tender part of a woman. We feel things there. We are vulnerable there. Something happened to me when she said that she had come close to harming

PART SEVEN

that part of her womanhood. I don't want it to happen to her. And I don't want it to happen to me.

PART SEVEN

Yes, I Do Have Feelings about That

I was introduced to *Mister Rogers' Neighborhood* late in life. My family physician told me that the only live, improvisational jazz piano he could hear on TV was on that show. My doctor was a sophisticated guy, so I was bemused by the idea that he would watch a TV show made for children. I tuned in right away, though. That was in 1983, and I've been a Fred Rogers fan ever since.

Aside from live music, Rogers had much to offer children of all ages. I was a 35-year-old working professional when I began watching the show, and I learned a lot from him. I'm 65 now, and what he taught me about feelings – in his calm, gentle way – is important for the intimacy I'm seeking as a mature woman.

Rogers died in 2003, and the book that came out that year, *The World According to Mister Rogers: Important Things to Remember*, has much to say about something I'm still working on: *feelings*.

Confronting our feelings and giving them appropriate expression always takes strength, not weakness. It takes strength to acknowledge our anger, and sometimes more strength yet to curb the aggressive urges that anger may bring, and to channel them into nonviolent outlets. It takes strength to face our sadness and to grieve and to let our grief and our anger flow in tears when they need to. It takes strength to talk about our feelings and to reach out for help and comfort when we need it.

And, as a person who now needs a walker to move around, I found this Rogers quote about disability to be insightful:

Part of the problem with the word 'disabilities' is that it immediately suggests an inability to see or hear or walk or do other things that many of us take for granted. But what of people who can't feel? Or talk about their feelings? Or manage their feelings in constructive ways? What of people who aren't able to form close and strong relationships? And people who cannot find fulfillment in their lives, or those who have lost hope, who live in disappointment and bitterness and find in life no joy, no love?

These, it seems to me, are the real disabilities.

Partnering for us as older adults might call on relationship skills we didn't develop when we were younger and more demanding. For example, where would we have learned how to talk with loved ones about our feelings? Most of us didn't learn it from our parents. We've seen intimate scenes in movies and on television shows, but when we put the intimate words into our own mouths, they sound fake. Maybe it's being vulnerable to feelings and to each other that will make the words sound less fake. Maybe being older will help us to *be* less fake.

Rogers wrote:

When we love a person, we accept him or her exactly as is the lovely with the unlovely, the strong along with the fearful, the true mixed in with the facade, and of course, the only way we can do it is by accepting ourselves that way.

I hear you, Mister Rogers. I hear you.

PART SEVEN

Are We Having Fun Yet?

I "borrowed" the *TIME* magazine from a year ago that I'd begun to read in my physical therapist's office. It was a special issue on health, and the cover promised that inside there would be "Dispatches from the Frontiers of Longevity."

A few days earlier, during the week I celebrated my 65th birthday, I spoke about longevity with three close friends who are healthy, unmarried, 70-year-old men. They each told me that in their remaining years they would do their best to *have fun.* They didn't necessarily use the word, *fun,* but they meant having *"a good life."* Only one of these friends is now retired, but each spoke about the future in a way that was different from the way we baby-boomers used to speak about the future – that is, before we knew we'd be living so long.

When we early baby-boomers were born in the late 1940s and 1950s, life expectancy for the average American was 70 years. Today, some of us might live to be 100, and might live for more than 30 years after retirement. When we started working back in the day, it was assumed that we'd stop working in our mid-60s, collect retirement benefits for a few years, and shortly thereafter, "kick the bucket."

Some of us even had a "bucket list" of things we wanted to do in retirement, but many of us did not. We were, after all, the children of folks who had lived through the Depression, and life had not been so easy for them. Social Security benefits had begun in 1935 but were not universal. Indeed, the idea of having a guaranteed income during one's old age was still a relatively new concept for our elders.

PART SEVEN

My father was a youth during the Depression. He was born in South Carolina in 1910 when life expectancy for a black man was about 36 years. One of the elders in his family, his Aunt Henrietta, told him about the importance of pensions when he was a teenager. She said that if he lived long enough to get one, he'd be set for life.

She also told him that the only prospects for a black man to get a pension in the then- segregated economy was by working 20 years for the railroad, or 20 years for the federal government. The jobs a black man could get back then – even ones with the railroad or the federal government – were physically hard, though. They were jobs that could take years off a man's life and make his retirement an iffy proposition.

My father's Aunt Henrietta would roll over in her grave if she knew that her grand- nephew would live to be 99, work for 20 years in an air-conditioned office for the City of New York, become a department manager, and collect retirement income from that job for over 40 years – twice as long as he worked there!

Perhaps because of Aunt Henrietta's early intervention, my father had a long to-do list when he retired at the age of 59: He finished his undergraduate degree; got a Masters; launched several businesses; started a nonprofit organization in Harlem; volunteered at his church and at senior centers; wrote and published a book; joined the NRA (go figure), and went to design school to learn how to make jewelry. In his way, I'm sure he had fun.

But his kind of fun is not necessarily what my baby-boomer friends have in mind.

Significantly, my father's generation still believed in the idea of hard work and a "work ethic," and would have had low regard for the fun-driven life my friends contemplate.

It was in his generation that the virtues of work morphed into the need for a virtuous life without work -- aka retirement.

Sociologist David Ekerdt coined the term, "busy ethic," in his 1986 article in The Gerontologist to characterize the way many people speak today about retirement. For Ekerdt, the busy ethic "esteems leisure that is earnest, occupied, and filled with activity." In his article, he writes:

The "busy ethic" is named after the common question put to people of retireable age, "What will you do (or are you doing) to keep yourself busy?" and their equally common reports that "I have a lot to keep me busy" and "I'm as busy as ever."

Just as there is a work ethic that holds industriousness and self-reliance as virtues, so, too, there is a "busy ethic" for retirement that honors an active life. It represents attempts to justify retirement in terms of the long-standing beliefs and values that belonged to our working life.

When I first heard my friends say that they wanted to have "fun," I reacted to them in the old-school way, too. I'm part of that multitude of people over 65 who got the "busy ethic" memo, too. My friends, I thought, were being shallow alpha males who just wanted to lie around in the sun all day like alpha lions on the Serengeti.

To be sure, Ekerdt acknowledges that the men in his surveys (more than the women) emphasized retirement as a time to have the freedom to enjoy life. But he goes on to say that the men surveyed also indicated that their leisure was responsibly busy.

The busy ethic, Ekerdt observed, "… tames the potentially unfettered pleasures of retirement to prevailing values about engagement that apply to adulthood."

But will the "busy ethic" tame us baby-boomers?

PART SEVEN

Remember, we're the "sex, drugs, and rock 'n' roll generation, and have always offered a stern critique of existing cultural norms. We've left an indelible mark on every stage of life we passed through, and I expect the same will be true for retirement.

It wasn't that long ago that the map of the life course did not include the stage we now call *retirement*. Society made provisions for it just as it accommodated in the early decades of the 20th century the stage, we call *adolescence*. Both appeared when social policy – labor laws, mandatory schooling, and New Deal legislation – brought big changes to our life expectations.

And now, we baby-boomers face a huge shift – not brought about by social policy this time, but by human biology. The challenge of living longer than we expected is demanding a lot of attention, and a lot of smart people have been thinking about it.

The article in TIME magazine that I mentioned earlier says that the culture guiding us today is "profoundly mismatched" to the length of the lives we are now living. The culture familiar to us tells us when to get an education, marry, have children, buy a house, work, and retire.

But it doesn't have to stay that way, the article says:

We might trade retirement for new models of working longer, so that parents can spend more time with young children, sabbaticals become more common and – imagine this – workers experience periods of leisure before old age.

An essential first step will be to change the way we think about our suddenly longer lives.

And that's where we baby-boomers come in.

When I think of the conversations I'm having with my friends about the next 30 years, we don't talk so much about "staying busy." We talk about having more life ahead of us than

PART SEVEN

we'd expected, and the fresh adventures we'd like to have. We talk about how technology is demanding that we look at the world in a different way. We talk about how much closer to us everything seems, and how much fun we had last night surfing the web.

We talk a lot about the newness of it all, and are grateful that life is, again, calling on our generation to address yet another new issue: What will it mean for an older adult to have a "good life?"

PART SEVEN

Finding the Butterfly Inside

*Children are caterpillars and adults are butterflies.
No butterfly ever remembers what it felt like being a caterpillar.*
  - **Cornelia Funke**

Last year, I attended a conference at Columbia University's Teachers College about the small, private school in Harlem I went to from kindergarten to eighth grade. The school was The Modern School and was headlined in the conference announcement as an example of early "progressive" education in the African American community. Modern School alumni were invited that day to be videotaped for an archival project underway at Teachers College, and asked to bring old photographs, report cards, and other ephemera that could be digitized for the project's website.

I saw schoolmates at the conference whom I hadn't seen in half a century. We reminisced about the school's food, childhood romances, disciplinarian teachers, annual festivals, and more. We sang the school song and summoned the names of schoolmates who weren't there that day. We laughed at the fact that we're now grandparents who collect pensions and retirement benefits. And we talked about how grateful we still are that our school's founder and visionary, Mildred Johnson, had insisted on excellence.

Back then, we were black kids who lived in a racially segregated world, and Mildred (we all called her by her first name) did her best to let the world know that *black kids are, indeed, excellent.* We believed her and took that belief with us everywhere we went.

PART SEVEN

When I got home after the conference, I thought about the many times in my adult life when I didn't feel so excellent. At such times, I would reflect on the "great potential" I'd had when I was young and wonder if I'd ever find the butterfly that lived inside me. During one of those periods in my late 40s, I bought a book called *Late Bloomers: 75 Remarkable People Who Found Fame, Success, and Joy in the Second Half of Their Lives.* I read it for reassurance that it wasn't too late for me – that I still had time.

I pulled the book off the shelf the other day to look at it again and see what it was saying. Its author, the late Brendan Gill, had been a writer at *The New Yorker Magazine* for more than 60 years, and was well-known in the arts and culture circles of New York City. Before I bought the book, though, I'd met him at an awards ceremony hosted by the Municipal Art Society in a Harlem Park to honor some Harlem community leaders. (Gill was a member of the Society's board of directors at the time.)

I was at the ceremony that day to accept an award from the Society on behalf of the Harlem nonprofit where I served on the board. The event's organizers had arranged to have each presenter and awardee sit next to each other, and I found myself seated next to Jacqueline Kennedy Onassis, the Municipal Art Society board member who would be presenting the award I was there to accept. As I sat in the hot sun that summer day, between Mrs. Onassis and opera legend, Jessye Norman, another awardee, my butterfly was nowhere to be seen; I felt small, outclassed, and inadequate.

In *Late Bloomers,* Brendan Gill writes that the process of growing up, like the process of growing old, is various and unpredictable. He assembles subjects for his book who are in their forties, fifties, sixties, seventies, and eighties, and says that the "lateness" he attaches to them doesn't have much to do with how many decades they have lived.

"Rather," he writes, "it has to do with the moment in time at which we discover, whether through an event dictated by forces outside ourselves, or by a seemingly spontaneous personal insight, some worthy means of fulfilling ourselves. The age at which we make this discovery is an irrelevance."

The book profiles such "late bloomers" as Julia Child, Colonel Sanders (Kentucky Fried Chicken), Ellen Stewart (Café LaMaMa), painters Paul Cezanne and Grandma Moses, and composers Charles Ives and Thelonious Monk. My favorite quotes in the book are from dog-whisperer, Barbara Woodhouse, who tells us that her life began at 70, and philanthropist, Brooke Astor, who says that she followed the caution her mother offered early: "Don't die guessing."

Others who have gained public recognition in late life might also come to mind. But the phenomenon of *achieving self-fulfillment* is the point of Gill's book. For him, late bloomers are the people who -- at whatever cost and under whatever circumstances -- have succeeded in finding themselves.

He writes:

To find oneself is plainly to have been lost. It is to have been stumbling about in a dark wood and to have encountered there, unexpectedly, and yet welcomely, a second self who is capable of leading one into the safety of a sunny upland meadow.

Stumbling about in a dark wood is exactly what life felt like to me during those times when I couldn't find my butterfly. Indeed, the "second self" Gill writes about may be the "secret sauce" of life. The second self may be the butterfly inside each of us that transforms itself from being a thing that crawls into a thing that flies.

I'm thinking now about all this because we baby-boomers are retiring at a time when we'll have to figure out what to do with the rest of our lives. We gave a lot of thought to work and career but didn't think much about what we wanted to do after we were done with those concerns.

When I talk to folks my age about life in retirement, we seem to be relying on such conventions as travel, study, hobbies, and volunteering as ways to fill up our days. What will we do with ourselves, though, when we become the first large generation of centenarians who have children as old as 80 and grandchildren as old as 60?

One of the quotes from *Late Bloomers* that moved me deeply was from the 19th century moral philosopher, Henri-Frederic Amiel, who illuminates our 21st century moment when he writes: *To know how to grow old is the master work of wisdom.* The knowledge we need now is one that our 20th century education -- no matter how progressive it might have been -- could not have foreseen: *It is the knowledge of how to grow old.*

Back in the day, people assumed we wouldn't be needing that kind of knowledge. We do, though. Our second selves' beckon. The butterfly inside is nudging us.

EPILOGUE

In the next several decades, we baby-boomers will pioneer a new world of intimacy. That world will be created from the possibilities and challenges we uncover as we live through the longer life expectancy that's been forecast for us.

Expressing mature intimacy and creating the closeness we yearn for will require us to build on some of the unique virtues we cultivated in our youth. The progressive attitudes and behaviors we embraced in the 1960s were enshrined in our generational anthem, *The Age of Aquarius:*

Harmony and understanding Sympathy and trust abounding No more falsehoods or derisions Golden living dreams of visions Mystic crystal revelation and the mind's true liberation Aquarius! Aquarius!

Ironically, our next frontier may find its early mapping in these sentiments and call on us to hear the old melody in a higher octave. If we rekindle the values expressed in that "anthem," we may find that what is attractive and lovable about us in our mature years is our expanded capacity to be grateful to life, open to change, and eager to welcome fresh pleasures. Fresh pleasures, indeed.

By unleashing our Age of Aquarius imagination, we may discover that we're unleashing a new appetite for pleasure -- one that allows us to savor deep intimacy as we navigate our way through our increased longevity.

Older adults today, studies show, don't think of intimacy as intercourse only, but, rather, view the sensation of feeling loved as caring tenderness, thoughtful appreciation, and sensitive attention. Having or being in an "intimate relationship" offers enjoyments that reward our sense of wellbeing and invite us to feel good about ourselves. We thrive when we feel loved.

Intimacy for us also happens in the relationships we have with siblings, friends, parents, children, and grandchildren, and others to whom we feel close. We know that these relationships, enhance our aliveness and help us to build resilience against life's challenges.

The mystic crystal revelation that lies ahead for those of us who are on the far side of 50 is the promise that deep intimacy and emotional closeness are portals to the life-affirming passions and pleasures that will uplift our hearts for as long as we live.

Milton Keynes UK
Ingram Content Group UK Ltd.
UKHW052119200324
439607UK00002B/7/J